TORY POLICY-MAKING: The Conservative Research Department 1929-2009

The Editor

Alistair Cooke is the official historian of the Conservative Party. He recently launched a new history section of the Party's official website to make information about Conservative leaders and their achievements available to a wider audience. He is also the official historian of the Carlton Club, and historical adviser to the Conservative Party Archive.

He edited and published a selection of the Conservative Research Department's records to mark its seventy-fifth anniversary in 2004. It is now available on the Party's website.

His recent publications include *The Carlton Club 1832-2007* (2007, with Sir Charles Petrie), *A Party of Change: A Brief History of the Conservatives* (2008) and *Tory Heroine: Dorothy Brant and the Rise of Conservative Women* (2008).

TORY POLICY-MAKING: The Conservative Research Department 1929-2009

EDITED BY ALISTAIR COOKE
WITH CONTRIBUTIONS FROM

David Cameron, Michael Dobbs, Oliver Letwin,
James O'Shaughnessy, Stephen Parkinson,
Chris Patten, and Brendon Sewill

© The contributors and the Conservative Research Department

All rights reserved.
No part of this book may be reprinted or reproduced or utilised in any form or by any electronic, mechanical, or other means, now known or hereafter invented, including photocopying and recording, or placed in any information or retrieval system, without permission in writing from the publisher.

Printed and published by
Manor Creative
7 & 8 Edison Road, Eastbourne, East Sussex, BN23 6PT
www.manorcreative.com

ISBN 13/978-1-905116-04-1

THIS BOOK

is dedicated to our founder's daughter-in-law,

Mrs Frank Chamberlain; his grand-daughter, Mary de Vere Taylor;

and to his great-grandson, Martin Harris,

who worked in the Conservative Research Department

at the start of his career

Contents

Editor's Preface

1. Introduction — Oliver Letwin … 1
2. 'Neville Chamberlain's Private Army' — Alistair Cooke … 5
3. Rab Butler's Golden Era? — Alistair Cooke and Stephen Parkinson … 27
4. Policy-Making for Heath — Brendon Sewill … 55
5. The Thatcher Years — Chris Patten … 79
6. Tradition and Change — David Cameron … 95
7. CRD under Cameron — James O'Shaughnessy … 101
8. Conclusion: An Extraordinary Political Backroom — Michael Dobbs … 107

Appendix 1:
Chairmen and Directors of the Conservative Research Department … 113

Appendix 2:
The Records of the Conservative Research Department … 115

Index … 117

Illustrations between pages 64 and 65

Note: Biographical details of contributors appear at the start of each chapter.

Editor's Preface

Guy Burgess applied for a post in it. Lord Longford was one of its founder members. Its first Director, Sir Joseph Ball, was a master of political dirty tricks who makes even the most accomplished of today's spin-doctors look like rank amateurs. Its ancestral spirits encourage the unconventional and the adventurous, as Matthew Parris's first fat volume of memoirs, *Chance Witness*, testify in only slightly exaggerated fashion. It was wholly appropriate that its first ever desk officer for the environment, appointed in 1969, should have been Boris Johnson's equally colourful father, Stanley.[1]

Those who love formal bureaucratic procedures and fixed routines have never found a happy home for themselves in the Conservative Research Department. But in return for a relaxed, congenial working environment the Department demands long hours, intense application and mastery of detail. The strange, but highly talented, little group that first occupied the CRD's original home in Old Queen Street in the 1930s was welded by Joseph Ball into a dedicated team in the service of their Chairman, Neville Chamberlain, as he pursued his quest for a Tory welfare state – a quest interrupted and slowed down, but not halted, by Hitler. The furious pace of politics today places even heavier demands on CRD's young men and women in 2009. Matthew Parris found CRD in the late 1970s 'a merry place', but only 'fitfully'.[2] The pressures thirty years later are intense and continuous; members of CRD are entitled to as much merriment as they can get by way of relief from them.

In this collection of essays a number of members of CRD, past and present, join me in discussing the role and character of the Department over the last eighty years. The period up to 1951 is covered by Stephen Parkinson and me as a straightforward historical exercise, drawing on both published works and the voluminous records of the Department in the Conservative Party Archive at the Bodleian Library in Oxford.[3] Thereafter the tone changes. The subsequent essays take the form of personal accounts of the work of the Department in various periods. Apart from David Cameron, who reflects on CRD's role in the Thatcher/Major era, all the contributors deal with years of Conservative opposition when the Research Department has the task of helping to prepare the Party for a return to government. It is in such periods that CRD performs its greatest services to the Party, and when those working in it find themselves thrust into the front line. 'You'll find it much more fun now they've got nobody to look after them', Ferdy Mount was told by a gleeful colleague after the Conservative defeat of 1964[4] – 'they' being the front bench who had lost their jobs and their civil servants. In such circumstances the pace of activity quickens and the importance of the work increases. The first-hand accounts included here show how it seemed at the time – after the defeats of 1964 and 1974 – and how it all seems now in 2009 after many years of opposition.

This is not an official Party publication: the views expressed in it are personal ones. Nor, obviously, is it a formal, detailed history of the Conservative Research Department. Such a history covering the first fifty years was published by John Ramsden nearly thirty years ago.[5] A very large collection of records for more recent years exists in the Conservative Party Archive where cataloguing, which has been constrained by limited (and voluntarily subscribed) funds, is now beginning.[6] In due course a new, full history will be possible. What this volume seeks to do is to bring CRD's history over the last eighty years to life through a series of vivid pen portraits by people who are, or have been, at the centre of the Department's work.

In London, where the contents of this book were assembled, I was fortunate to have the assistance of Stephen Parkinson. In Eastbourne, where this book was printed, I had the benefit once again of the skills of my old friend Nigel Day and his kind colleagues at Manor Creative. I am very grateful to them all.

ALISTAIR COOKE
11 September 2009

[1] He got the job after writing out of the blue to Ted Heath asking if there was 'anything I could do to help remove Harold Wilson from office and help the Conservatives return to power' (Stanley Johnson, *Stanley I Presume*, Fourth Estate, 2009, p. 234). I offered Boris a job in 1988, but he preferred journalism.

[2] Matthew Parris, *Chance Witness: An Outsider's Life in Politics* (Viking, 2002), p. 177.

[3] A note on these records by Jeremy McIlwaine, the Party's Archivist, can be found on p. 115.

[4] Ferdinand Mount, *Cold Cream: My Early Life and Other Mistakes* (Bloomsbury, 2008), p. 267. Douglas Hurd, however, who joined the Department in 1966 found that 'they' needed comparatively little from him: 'we produced a dull little review of world affairs, and briefing papers as needed by our front bench' (Douglas Hurd, *Memoirs*, paperback edition, 2003, p. 187 where he misnumbers 34 Old Queen Street as 38).

[5] John Ramsden, *The Making of Conservative Party Policy: The Conservative Research Department since 1929* (Longman, 1980).

[6] See p. 116 for details.

Oliver Letwin
INTRODUCTION

OLIVER LETWIN dealt with education issues in CRD in 1982–83 while also working as Special Adviser to Sir Keith Joseph, then Secretary of State for Education. He was a major contributor to The Campaign Guide 1983 *and co-editor of the Department's* Daily Notes *during the 1983 election campaign. He became Chairman of the Department, and of David Cameron's Policy Review, in December 2005.*

Plenty of organisations from universities to pharmaceutical companies depend on research for their survival. Academic research in its proper sense – the unrestricted investigation of the unknown – is part of their reason for existence. Political Parties are not in this category. The unrestricted investigation of the unknown is not their strength and it is not their purpose.

In industrial terms, political Parties are directed towards development rather than research. Or in more cultural and less flattering terms, political Parties are ruthless users of ideas rather than giants of intellectual originality. No surprise, then, that when I first applied to join the Conservative Research Department, I was disabused of any pretences. The first words spoken to me by Peter Cropper, the enigmatic and brilliant Director, left the matter in no doubt: 'you must understand that the one thing the Conservative Research Department does not do, is research'.

This begs the question: why does a political Party, which is not an academic or scientific organisation, require a research department at all? The real answer lies in the historical record – the changing but persistently important specific contributions made by the Research

Department that are charted in the essays that follow. Indeed, the provision of that textured, historical answer is the main point of this collection so admirably gathered together by the Department's doyen, Alistair Cooke.

But it is perhaps useful to try to draw out at least the semblance of a general answer at the level of crude theory – to try to identify what a research department that does not do academic research can contribute to a political Party that has to engage with the issues of the day and the hour. This way of putting the question already suggests an important part of the answer.

A great, democratic political Party is constantly engaged in the media mêlée. It has an annual general meeting every day of the year. To prevent itself being in the long run destroyed by this inevitable preoccupation with the immediate, it needs some group of people who are to a degree removed from the mêlée. But, to fulfil their rescue-mission, these people cannot simply be sequestered in academic reflection. If they are to make contact with the front line of politics, they must engage with events. They need, in other words, to occupy a space between the rough and tumble of sheer electoral politics and the calm waters of the intellect.

It is this space between intellect and politics that the Conservative Research Department has occupied throughout its history.

*

This shouldn't for a moment be confused with any suggestion that the Research Department is, or has ever been, an ideological pressure group. On the contrary, it has been distinct at all times from the many pressure groups and think-tanks that have from time to time constituted a part of the Conservative family or have exerted influence over the Conservative Party.

It was, indeed, for that very reason that Geoffrey Howe and William Rees-Mogg established the Bow Group in the 1950s, Keith Joseph and Margaret Thatcher created the Centre for Policy Studies in the 1970s, and – most recently – Francis Maude and Archie Norman set up Policy Exchange. In each case, the founders had an avowed intent to pursue an ideological agenda rather than a Party agenda; and in each case, they correctly recognised that the Research Department of the Party was not the right instrument.

The Research Department is – at any given time – a civil service for the Leader and Cabinet or Shadow Cabinet, avowedly partisan on behalf of the Party but not factional or ideological within the Party. This, in turn, implies that the tone and character of the Research Department's approach at any given time is defined by the strategy of the Party leadership. And, because of the nature of British Conservatism, that means change over time.

As Brendon Sewill makes clear in his essay, 'Conservative principles, and in those days we quoted a good deal of Burke and Disraeli, are sufficiently broad to cover almost any policy'. In true Burkean fashion, the Conservative Party has changed, as the country it seeks to govern has changed. Indeed, the ability to change has ironically been one of the great constants throughout the Conservative Party's long and distinguished history.

At each turn, as the Party has defined and redefined itself in opposition to the various heresies with which it has been presented – from Clause 4 socialism to New Labour's deficit bureaucracy – the Research Department (and, in times of government, the Special Advisers associated with it) have provided not the map, but the engine and the gears that have enabled the leadership to translate general direction into specific programme. And, of course, although this does not involve unrestricted research, it does involve analysis – because the space between politics and intellect is not a void. It is occupied by rigorous analysis of the actual effects of the policies of opponents, of the true state of the administration, and of the impacts of proposed or possible Party policy.

So, if names were chosen for accuracy rather than continuity, we would call the CRD not the Research Department but the Analysis Department.

*

But even that, more accurate name would miss part of the point – because the CRD is not, and has never been, just an apparatus with a contemporary purpose. It is also, and has always been, in part a breeding-ground for the future leadership of the Party.

One of the reasons why the Department's specific role and character have been so able to change repeatedly is that it has never been institutionalised. Unlike the rest of what is now known as Conservative Campaign Headquarters, the Research Department is not, and has never been, a servant of the Party apparatus as a whole. It answers to the leader, and its members have always had direct access to (and have always been closely connected with) the politicians who form the Cabinet or Shadow Cabinet.

Because of that direct access, because of its analytical role midway between politics and the intellect, and because of its notoriously modest pay and lack of internal career prospects, it has persistently attracted to its ranks a particular kind of people: young people of high intelligence who are willing to work for much less than they could earn elsewhere because of their interest in the substance of policy.

As a result – in contrast to its German counterpart, the Konrad-Adenauer-Stiftung – the CRD has never become a hierarchy. It has always been, instead, a collection of talented young impresarios, contributing intellectual energy to the Party while acquiring for themselves a knowledge of policy and high politics on their way to something else. And this, no doubt, is why, from Maudling to Cameron, the Department has been one of the ports of call in the careers of so many of the most serious Conservative politicians.

*

All of this – the involvement in an activity of pragmatic analysis that is neither pure research nor pure politics, the relentless refusal to be imprisoned in a narrow ideology, and the ingenious ability to attract and train people of real quality at a low cost through adopting a non-bureaucratic style – is at once very English, very Oakeshottian and very Conservative.

Only the Conservative Party could have invented the Conservative Research Department.

Alistair Cooke
'NEVILLE CHAMBERLAIN'S PRIVATE ARMY'

ALISTAIR COOKE joined the Conservative Research Department in May 1977 to work for Airey Neave on Northern Ireland policy. He was first Assistant, and then Deputy, Director between 1983 and 1997; he was also Director of the Conservative Political Centre. He edited the publications of both organisations, producing six editions of The Campaign Guide: *a seventh followed in 2005 after his return to the Department as a consultant. His chief interest today is his work as a historian of the Conservative Party. His recent publications include* The Carlton Club 1832–2007 *(with Sir Charles Petrie).*

> Neville Chamberlain has died, a good man whose merits will be better appreciated in the future (Viscount Mersey's Diary, 13 November 1940, printed in his *Journals and Memories*, John Murray, 1952, p. 5).

Will Viscount Mersey's prediction ever come true? Nearly seventy years after his death, Neville Chamberlain's merits still remain largely unrecognised. He continues to attract almost unremitting public obloquy. Churchill is synonymous with national glory, Chamberlain with ignominy. Appeasement, whose lasting stigma doomed the Conservative Party (despite Churchill's subsequent 'cleansing' leadership) to defeat at the 1945 election[1], has obliterated the memory of his remarkable social reforms of the 1920s and 1930s which made him a dominant figure in inter-war politics. People seem unwilling to accept that a politician can be a brilliant success in one area while coming badly to grief in another. One simple, overall judgement is pronounced – with greater vehemence when, as in Chamberlain's case, some sort of fundamental moral error is thought to have been committed. At least the rather mindless vehemence of the condemnation can now be corrected at long last, thanks to the brilliant account of Chamberlain's appeasement policies, based on all the relevant sources, published by David Faber last year[2] which provides the first full impartial explanation of the varied strategic and political factors which led Chamberlain reluctantly to Munich.

Chamberlain took up foreign affairs when he became Prime Minister in 1937 at the age of sixty-eight because Hitler, by raising the stakes so high, gave him little option. Until then, his life had been dominated by a powerful sense of mission, apparent from his time as a highly successful Lord Mayor of Birmingham during the First World War, to give fuller effect to one of the great aims that Disraeli had set for the Conservative Party: the elevation of the condition of the people. 'I believe', he told the eloquent, but sleepy Stanley Baldwin in November 1924, 'I may do something to improve the condition for the less fortunate classes – and that's after all what we are in politics for'.[3] That same month he matched his words with deeds, putting a programme of twenty-five measures of social improvement before Baldwin as the latter formed what was to become (thanks to Chamberlain) one of the great reforming governments of the twentieth century.[4] Twenty-one of the proposals had been implemented by the time Baldwin and Chamberlain, one of the most effective partnerships for good in modern history, lost power at the election of May 1929. The long list of changes had several striking features. Contributory pensions had been introduced, the foundations had been laid for a national health service, the largest house-building programme of the century had been started, and the old Victorian system of local government had been replaced by a new structure. The welfare state had advanced significantly.

People loved working for Neville Chamberlain. He was the hero of Whitehall. To the formidable head of the civil service, Warren Fisher, he was 'darling Neville' until appeasement policies brought deep disillusionment. Chamberlain vies with Margaret Thatcher for the title of the hardest-working peace-time Prime Minister of modern times. Paper flowed briskly to and from his desk. He got things done.

Even after losing the premiership in the most humiliating circumstances in May 1940, he remained a master of public business. 'The superior administrative capacity of Neville Chamberlain', a leading economist later recalled writing of his last months, made him 'the one Minister in this field from whom you could get clear and immediate directives'.[5] Churchill, who was later to do so much to keep Chamberlain's reputation at rock bottom when he came to write his war memoirs, had earlier looked forward to a close war-time partnership with him. 'What shall I do without poor Neville?', he asked on Chamberlain's death. 'I was relying on him to look after the Home Front for me.'[6] Indeed, the home front in British politics has never known a more formidable figure than Neville Chamberlain. Some complained that his dedication to duty made him joyless and intimidating. Others were surprised that he remained a convivial figure, despite the long hours of work. One backbench Conservative MP wrote in 1926 that he 'is not boring despite his amazing efficiency and complete mastery over subjects which to me are boring *à mourir*'.[7]

When Chamberlain first became the Tories' indefatigable chief policy-maker in the 1920s, he swiftly concluded that arrangements needed to be made so that serious preparatory work for government could be done under the Party's aegis. The electorate of over twenty-one million created in 1918 was almost three times larger than it had been before the First World War. In the new era of mass democracy, political parties needed to devise programmes for government. Baldwin did not agree. He believed that incoming ministers should present their civil servants with an idea or two and leave them to get on with it, just as they had always done. Election manifestos had customarily contained a few short, often fairly bland paragraphs: they should continue to do so. Chamberlain did not find it easy to get his way. Progress was made, and then unmade. Assisted by a little secretariat set up on an *ad hoc* basis by the Shadow Cabinet in 1924 when the Party was briefly in opposition during the first Labour ministry, Chamberlain prepared and published a full programme for government entitled *Looking Ahead*. It 'provided the Party with a comprehensive and practicable statement of its policies for the first time ever, and made the provision of an election manifesto a few months later an easy task'.[8] The manifesto, which did not greatly exceed Baldwin's preferred length, heralded the major social reforms passed by his government of 1924–9, but he saw no need to repeat the exercise. The manifesto for the 1929 election was cobbled together by civil servants without the benefit of Chamberlain's firm, directing hand. Muddled and uninspiring though it was, it ran ironically to twice as many pages as its effective 1924 predecessor. Baldwin's indifference cost him the brevity to which he had long been so attached.

The crushing election defeat of May 1929, in which the Party lost over a hundred seats, finally put paid to the old, simple ways favoured by Baldwin. He had been advised often enough by serious-minded colleagues that he would have to change. Leo Amery, his Colonial Secretary who loved putting ideas, particularly imperial ideas, into effect, told him shortly after the 1924 victory that 'the Party should be preparing a programme for the future … The idea that the Party in office can rely for its materials for preparing the political campaign upon departmental officials or upon the Cabinet Secretariat is, we think, wholly erroneous'.[9] John Buchan, the prolific best-selling novelist and high-minded political thinker, was among those who joined the growing chorus for change, calling in 1928 for 'Political Research work, for which we have the machinery sketched out, and which badly needs undertaking'.[10] When in 1929 Baldwin was finally forced to succumb, his most faithful acolyte, J. C. C. Davidson (a man always known by his initials), who happened to be Party Chairman at the time, declared very usefully, and quite correctly, that he had long favoured the creation of a Party research department.* He now swiftly acquired resources and premises for it. He believed that 'it should be financially

---

*In his great classic work *The Conservative Party from Peel to Thatcher* (Fontana paperback, 1990, p. 260), Robert Blake states that the Conservative Research Department was 'founded by Davidson'. Davidson himself made no such claim. His contribution was limited to the provision of premises and funds when Baldwin finally accepted the case for establishing a research department (see John Ramsden, *The Making of Conservative Party Policy: The Conservative Research Department since 1929*, Longman, 1980, p. 38).

independent of the Central Office, and the problem was met when a prominent supporter gave the necessary finance; as a result 24 Old Queen Street was acquired and maintained without any call upon Central Office funds'.[11]

No great fanfare greeted the birth of the Conservative Research Department. The details of the new arrangements were made clear in a press statement issued quietly on 17 November 1929. 'In view of the growing complexity of the political aspect of modern industrial, Imperial and social problems, Mr Stanley Baldwin has decided to set up a special department charged with the task of organising and conducting research into these matters'.[12] The statement went on to explain that Lord Eustace Percy had been given the job of establishing it. Chamberlain was not immediately available: he was about to depart on a three-month visit to Africa, his first proper holiday for years. Percy, a former Education Minister who had strong intellectual credentials (he ended up as a university vice-chancellor) was a mere stop-gap, as he made clear in his memoirs. He accepted the temporary post 'at Baldwin's rather half-hearted request as a preliminary job of survey and organisation, on the understanding that the department would be taken over by Neville Chamberlain on his return from abroad'. Percy departed as soon as Chamberlain got back: 'he gave me clearly to understand that he did not want me to have any more to do with it'.[13]

At first Whitehall was distinctly unimpressed by the new arrival. 'Eustace Percy has been made head of some sort of research group at the Tory central office', the Deputy Cabinet Secretary, Thomas Jones, noted rather dismissively on 23 December 1929.[14] All that changed the moment Chamberlain formally took over as Chairman in March 1930 just as the Department was about to move from temporary offices in Victoria Street into its new Old Queen Street home, overlooking St James's Park and a few minutes' walk from the House of Commons. The new political platoon was to remain under his exclusive command until his death in November 1940, proud to be known as 'Neville Chamberlain's private army' and achieving considerable political significance as a result. Chamberlain himself wrote in March 1930 that 'I found things rather a mess ... but there is a different atmosphere now and they are all rather excited and feeling that they are going to be an important body. I am getting very much interested myself and it seems to me that through my new Department I shall have my finger on the springs of policy'.[15] Already dominant in Whitehall, Chamberlain now had in the Conservative Research Department the means to exercise full control over the Party's preparatory work for government just at the moment when it had become universally agreed that sustained political research was needed if Conservative governments were to thrive. He used his Department to help secure a second phase of far-reaching reform in the 1930s, extending further his successes of the 1920s. Baldwin remained Leader until 1937, but all significant power over Conservative domestic policy now rested with Neville Chamberlain. But for Hitler, the 1930s would have come to be regarded by Conservative historians as the apotheosis of Neville Chamberlain, assisted by his private army.

*

The CRD army was very small, numbering no more than eight in all, including three secretaries. The Director of the Department throughout the Chamberlain years, Joseph Ball, who was knighted for his services in 1936, was a man who played many roles, most of them carefully hidden from view. He was one of MI5's most successful and least scrupulous officers both before and during his CRD years. J. C. C. Davidson, Baldwin's faithful Party Chairman, who recruited Ball as the Party's first Director of Publicity in 1927, described him as a man who 'has had as much experience as anyone I know in the seamy side of life and the handling of crooks'.[16] That rather suggests that he had just a good knowledge of the underworld of knaves and rascals. In fact the country possessed no greater expert. Lacking any kind of moral compass, there was quite literally no misdeed to which he himself was not prepared to stoop. He makes Alastair Campbell in our own day look rather like a sea-green incorruptible.

His was a life lived carefully in separate compartments (which I intend to open in a future publication), and his CRD colleagues knew nothing of his total disregard of all legal niceties in other aspects of his activities, though they probably guessed that there was much more to him than met the eye. But what they encountered in the Research Department was an extraordinarily able administrator and a possessor of formidable political judgement. His efficiency and skill made him a man after Neville Chamberlain's own heart. In their lengthy and fascinating correspondence, Chamberlain's 'My dear Ball' gave way in the late 1930s to 'My dear Joseph', an honour which that reserved and undemonstrative Prime Minister accorded to very few. Chamberlain knew that he could rely on Ball to ensure that CRD produced work of the highest quality on time whenever he required it, and at some point he discovered some of Ball's other compartments too: they were to prove very useful to him as he prosecuted his appeasement policies after 1937 by all possible means, both within and beyond the normal political processes.[17]

Two promising young intellectuals were Ball's chief associates in setting and maintaining high standards in the CRD. The first was none other than the future Lord Longford, Labour Cabinet Minister and much else besides, who as Frank Pakenham was then undecided as between a career as an Oxford academic or Tory politician. He left CRD in 1932 (after marrying the radical Elizabeth Harman, a cousin of Chamberlain and, later, aunt of Harriet) for a post in the newly established Economic Advisory Council: four years later he was struck on the head during a riot in Oxford fomented by Mosley's Blackshirts, an event which some uncharitably associated with the start of a new susceptibility to left-wing and other influences. His three years in CRD saw him involved in projects to promote political education through a Tory equivalent to the left-wing Workers' Educational Association (WEA) as well as in weighty research subjects, though afterwards he claimed to have spent much of his time reading French novels.

Pakenham gave fervent expression to a strong social conscience that was already a marked feature of his character. Sorely provoked in argument with 'a socialist female don who looked as she had never left a convent in her life ... I could not help pointing out that for the last five years I had slept on average two nights a week in the East

End of London'. He believed that 'the Conservative ideal should be one of the working classes asking to be taught to think, and of those more fortunate in their educational opportunities hurrying to teach them'.[18] To that end Pakenham drew up detailed 'proposals for a scheme of Conservative education' in January 1932 under which constituency committees would organise lectures and classes with the clear aim of extending support for the Party among the working classes.[19] Ball hoped (in vain as it turned out) that the Party would 'turn to account the unique knowledge possessed by Mr Pakenham'.[20] When serious political education finally got under way at constituency level with the establishment in 1945 of the Conservative Political Centre (CPC) by Rab Butler (to work in close partnership with the Research Department), it had the more limited objective of equipping existing Party members with a better understanding of Conservative policy.

Pakenham's principal colleague, Henry Brooke, another Oxford star, was an altogether more staid individual with an immense appetite for work. He produced long, impressive, clearly written papers and reports on almost all the subjects dealt with in the 1930s at Chamberlain's request. One month it might be unemployment benefit; the next, trends in world trade; a third, agriculture. Almost every file of CRD papers for these years in the Conservative Party Archive is adorned by one of Brooke's extraordinary range of contributions. Chamberlain commended him warmly. In a typical expression of satisfaction with Brooke's work made in a letter to Ball in 1933 he described a memorandum on work-sharing as 'worth a hundred of the Ministry of Labour's document. Brooke's paper really puts facts, and shows the difficulties very well',[21] providing Chamberlain with just what he needed to raise the issue with the Prime Minister, Ramsay MacDonald.

A year spent in a Quaker settlement for the unemployed in the Rhondda Valley before joining the CRD had instilled in Brooke a deep commitment to economic and social progress which made him a natural Chamberlain man*: and, like Chamberlain and Ball, he enjoyed asking the tough questions about how progress could be

---

*Footnote opposite.

achieved within an evolving framework of Tory policy which allotted no place to high taxation as the basis for extended state activity. One answer was what came to be known later as regional policy – action by the state to encourage industry to relocate to unemployment blackspots like south Wales. In a neat little exercise, characteristic of them, Chamberlain and Ball arranged for Brooke to be commissioned by *The Times* in March 1934 to write a series of anonymous articles on the miserable conditions in 'Places without a Future' where it seemed that only state intervention could reverse decline. Chamberlain was delighted with the results, praising the articles as 'brilliantly written and full of ideas'. They provided 'the impetus for the development of Britain's first attempt at regional policy' by enabling Chamberlain 'to force the pace of reform upon reluctant colleagues'[22] – a trick that he used the press to help him perform on other occasions, including, most controversially, over appeasement. In 1934 the collusion between Chamberlain, Ball, Brooke and *The Times* led to the Special Areas Act under which the first direct efforts were made – albeit in tentative form – to assist parts of the country that ordinary market forces could never rescue. (No less helpful to Chamberlain was another series of anonymous articles in the summer of 1938 written by Brooke, giving a first-hand account of conditions in Germany where he stayed with friends, 'presumably Dawson, editor of *The Times,* having been persuaded to accept them by Ball'.[23])

Brooke was the linchpin of the Research Department until his departure in 1937 to prepare for a Parliamentary career which eventually brought about the near-destruction of his reputation when he became an extraordinarily accident-prone Home Secretary in the early 1960s. Clever intellectuals are often unsuited to the hurly-burly of practical politics. Pakenham's successor in Chamberlain's private army, David Clarke, a Cambridge man at last,

---

*As a result Churchill took strongly against him, and in 1944 spent an hour and a half berating his Chief Whip for 'boosting his enemies' when he recommended 'that very able young man Henry Brooke' for a junior government post (John Barnes and David Nicholson (eds.), *The Empire at Bay: The Leo Amery Diaries 1929-1945*, Hutchinson, 1988, p. 991).

who had an extremely fine mind, resisted all efforts to persuade him to go into Parliament.

Ball, Brooke and Clarke established CRD extremely successfully under the terms that Chamberlain had laid down at the start: 'we shall be at once an Information Bureau providing data and briefs for leaders, and a long term Research body'.[24] Another of the pioneers, Henry Stannard, ensured that it would not be a solemn or pompous body, but one that would always relish the kind of eccentricity that he himself first imparted to it. In one of his many books of reminiscence, Frank Longford recalled Stannard with considerable affection as a man who, after successes at Oxford including the presidency of the Union, 'had not quite succeeded in life'. He showed his very odd character which endeared him to Longford when Chamberlain paid them a visit in their room in Old Queen Street:

> Neville Chamberlain showed every desire to put us at our ease. In a dead silence he walked over to the window, gazed across the park for a moment, appeared to be thinking hard for something to say, and then threw out the gambit: 'I wonder if those trees are cherry trees?' Stannard drew himself up to his full five feet three inches. 'All trees', he remarked in his old-fashioned Union manner, 'are cherry trees'. Chamberlain looked at him, puzzled. 'Surely', he said, 'that's rather an exaggeration'. 'All truth', said Stannard, still more pontifically, 'is an exaggeration'. Chamberlain seemed to ponder this one deeply. He frowned, less it seemed in rejection than in genuine bewilderment. He left the room with no further word spoken on either side, and never visited us upstairs again.[25]

Stannard's irreverence might have been a bit extreme but it was not untypical. From that day to this the Department's members have rejected stuffiness and gravity as appropriate accompaniments of their hard work in favour of humour and light-heartedness. CRD has always been very, very unlike a government department.

Even the less intellectually stimulating aspects of its activities – particularly work on solid literature for Conservative candidates to use – failed to dampen the mood. From its inception CRD had responsibility for ensuring that Conservative policy was accurately explained to those who had to propound it publicly. 'Blue bibles', known in the 1930s as election *Handbooks* rather than *Campaign Guides* (the older title reappeared in 1950), were produced by Central Office to tell candidates – at least those of them who could read* – all that the Party leadership thought they should know. Ball and his team checked the contents, without venturing much into the actual drafting, as their successors were to do after 1945. But during the election campaigns of the 1930s CRD's actual words were dispatched to Parliamentary candidates and constituencies bringing them sharp lines of attack on the other Parties and incisive information to answer all manner of questions from inquisitive electors and to reply to the formal questionnaires from the Esperanto Society and other organisations which pestered candidates for statements of Tory policy in their recondite areas. The pattern of the Department's electoral activity, familiar to all who have worked in it during general election campaigns, was settled at the very start. Ball also began the practice of helping the Party's leaders with political broadcasts, telling Baldwin's PPS in 1931 that 'the Research Department will be ready and willing to collaborate'[26] in their preparation, setting another trend for his successors to follow.

*

The creation of the Research Department in 1929 coincided with the onset of a world economic crisis (which struck Britain in its most virulent form in 1931) and with a period of extraordinary turmoil in the Conservative Party following its severe election defeat, which almost toppled Baldwin. At one point he seriously contemplated

---

*'Chips' Channon who kept the best political diary of the period recorded the following anecdote on 20 February 1934: 'James Willoughby told me today that he nearly gave up his parliamentary campaign in November, as he just could not stand the ordeal of speaking: when he confessed this to his agent, the man replied, "Don't let not speaking well dishearten you: I have known candidates who could not even read"' (R. R. James (ed.), *'Chips': The Diaries of Sir Henry Channon*, Weidenfeld paperback, 1993, p. 16).

resigning his seat and fighting a by-election in an effort to restore his severely shaken authority. It fell to Chamberlain to end the crisis. He devised the means of restoring unity under Baldwin. His plan involved the ending of free trade and the introduction of tariffs. This was nothing new. It was widely seen as the obvious course for the son of Joseph Chamberlain who had launched his great crusade for just that purpose almost thirty years earlier. Since then, the Party had suffered agonies of internal discord on the issue and Neville Chamberlain, an infinitely more flexible (and therefore more successful) politician than his father, had for much of the time concentrated on other things, invoking Disraeli to sanctify his great measures of social reform in the 1920s. Now he sensed that tariff reform, so long a source of internal Tory strife, could actually be a healing force, as well as a crucial component of an economic policy designed to restore Britain's prosperity (for which he would be severely taken to task both at the time and later by Keynesians and all those who believe that expansionist policies and sustained measures of international co-operation are the ways to beat economic recession*).

On the Party point, Chamberlain was absolutely right. Protection fused most of the warring elements together in 1931. Very conveniently, he now had his new Department to work out the details for him. A grand Committee of assorted *eminenti* deliberated in the first half of 1931 with the ubiquitous Brooke as their secretary. After twenty-five meetings held in Old Queen Street, they presented their report of over a hundred closely typed pages on 24 June 1931. 'The Committee have tried to construct as simple a tariff as possible, on general and readily intelligible principles'.[27] Brooke commented

---

*Chamberlain gave his critics short shrift with the aid of Treasury calculations in 1937 which showed that the Americans under Roosevelt 'have secured an appreciable improvement in employment, it is true; and in the process have increased their national debt by 17,000 million dollars. We have secured greater improvement, without adding to the debt at all' (Robert Self, *Neville Chamberlain: A Biography*, Ashgate Publishing Limited, 2006, p. 207). With Chamberlain's policies of tariffs and balanced budgets, Britain achieved annual average growth of 2.3 per cent in the 1930s, just behind Social Democrat Sweden where a fiscal stimulus produced growth of 2.6 per cent, as the Conservative historian Graham Stewart pointed out in *The Times* on 14 March 2009.

privately that apart from the chairman, Philip Cunliffe-Lister (later Lord Swinton) 'none of the other members seemed really to understand what it was all about'.[28] But it provided Chamberlain with what he wanted. The Department, he wrote five days later, 'has now worked out pretty completely the arrangements for an early imposition of an emergency tariff; the procedure for getting it through Parliament as quickly as possible; and the setting up of a Tariff Commission or Board, to administer it, and to carry out subsequent adjustments'. As a result 'we shall be able, if and when we are returned to office, to bring the Tariff into operation with the minimum of delay'.[29] Thus the Conservative-dominated National Government formed by Ramsay MacDonald in August 1931 with Chamberlain as Chancellor of the Exchequer obtained a key element of its programme from the Department. It was a notable coup for the infant institution.

Tariffs worked as a unifying force among Conservatives in part because they made it possible to introduce a system of imperial preference demanded by some of Baldwin's most ardent Tory critics. Here the Department had gone into action a year earlier, with Brooke and Pakenham working in tandem in 1930 without the encumbrance of any form of committee. Their extensive joint report delighted Ball on his return from his summer holiday. 'My dear Brooke', he wrote on 5 September 1930, 'I have deferred writing to you until I had had an opportunity of reading your memorandum on the trade of the Empire, which I found waiting for me … it will prove of the utmost value to the Department and the Party Leaders'. He went on to note 'the great opportunity which awaits our manufacturers', particularly in Canada while, with his usual acumen, pinpointing what was to prove a source of lasting frustration to Tory policy-makers over the years: 'the difficulty which the Party is faced with is that of persuading the leaders of many of our principal industries that they have really got to go out after business as the American manufacturer does'.[30] As the 1930s wore on, Ball was to receive many tiresome representations from businessmen (being the perfect spy he had contacts everywhere) who wanted increased protection for their products in the home market to save themselves the effort of promoting them vigorously abroad.

The Department acquired formidable expertise in all aspects of imperial trade, carefully studying trends in the self-governing Dominions and the dependent colonies, as many bulky files among its records at the Bodleian testify. Ball himself worked closely and in considerable secrecy (as he loved to do) with Samuel Hoare, Secretary of State for India, on the possibilities of increasing British exports to India. Hoare sent Ball 'very confidential' information which 'it would no doubt be very embarrassing to the Board of Trade if it were known ... I hope it will enable you to develop the work which you did previously'.[31]

Ball journeyed to the most famous of all Imperial Conferences held in Ottawa in July 1932 as part of the British delegation led by Baldwin (but with Chamberlain of course doing all the work) to establish the new tariff arrangements designed to unite Britain closely with its Empire. The experience destroyed Chamberlain's faith in his father's great plan for Britain's imperial destiny. 'Whilst Britain agreed measures designed to help Dominion agricultural penetration of her own market, no real attempt was made by the Dominions to make it easier in return for British exports to enter their markets'.[32]

The Research Department was given the job of monitoring the various (and often one-sided) agreements made at Ottawa. ' My dear Butler', wrote Ball to the CRD's future Chairman, then the junior minister at the India Office, in 1936, 'we have been charged by Mr Neville Chamberlain with the task of preparing memoranda on the Ottawa Agreements'[33]. Would Butler kindly send a proof copy of his forthcoming report on trade with India? (Butler, as it happened, would not.) This was rarely rewarding work. By 1938 David Clarke had seen so much evidence of the Dominions' narrow devotion to their own self-interests that he began to wonder whether 'the UK Government ought to be free to impose duties upon imports of manufactured goods from the Dominions and India'.[34] Disillusionment with the whole Ottawa system of imperial preference spread far and wide. One of the wealthiest men in the country, Lord Bute, made clear his deep discontent to the Liberal peer, Lord Mersey, as war loomed. 'Bute, a Tory and a great landowner, considers that the Ottawa Conference is responsible for our troubles. General feeling is, I believe, moving that way'.[35]

Because of the importance attached to it as a political issue, imperial trade remained one of the Department's principal concerns throughout the 1930s. It was also constantly alert to the possibilities of improving the general tariff policy which it had given the Party. Other tasks came and went in the early 1930s, none more important than inquiries into dealing with the huge cost placed on public spending by high unemployment.[36] In 1933 the Department devised a detailed scheme for the complete reorganisation of the coal industry which, after immense controversy, was finally implemented in 1938, giving the state a permanent role in the industry's affairs.[37]

Ball sought a more ambitious basis for the Department's operations in the years ahead. He got it at the end of January 1934 when Chamberlain arrived at Old Queen Street one day to say that he 'wanted to set to work on a new programme'.[38] Ball's note on the meeting records that Chamberlain suggested three main topics: '1. The creation of a Ministry of Defence, absorbing the War Office, Admiralty and Air Ministry. (He had some doubt whether much economy could be effected by this proposal.) 2. The future relations between the state and industry. 3. Work-sharing schemes (Hitler and N. R. A. and overtime)'. Ball himself added no less than fourteen more topics including 'more stringent control over the press' (no doubt to help him avoid journalistic prying into his darker side which occasionally nearly caused serious scandal), the creation of an impartial Imperial and Economic Statistical Bureau, profit-sharing in industry, a supplementary pensions scheme, a new phase of the Tory house-building programme to provide one million low-rent homes and, most remarkably, 'the serious state of the nation's physique, and the possibility of taking advantage of the urge among the young for physical training, by linking a scheme with the Party Organisation'.[39] (One almost expects the words 'Chamberlain Youth' to appear.)

Ball, notoriously unfit himself, had hit on an idea that proved immensely attractive to Chamberlain and his colleagues. It became one of the Research Department's priority areas when a Cabinet

Conservative Committee (CCC) consisting of all the Tory Ministers in the National Government was set up shortly afterwards with Ball as its secretary and Old Queen Street as its meeting place in order 'to map out our programme (1) to the election, (2) to go the country with', in Chamberlain's words.[40] Baldwin, sceptical as always about policy-making in the Party, often could not be bothered to attend: in one of his two recorded contributions to the Committee's discussions he averred that 'no greater service could be performed by the Government than to teach the people what to eat and how to cook it'.[41]

Chamberlain kept all the Committee's work firmly in his own hands, assisted zealously by Ball. Disregarding Baldwin's little comments on diet, Chamberlain stressed that he wanted 'a comprehensive policy for the improvement of the health and physique of the nation ... he thought the Government should concentrate on closing the existing gaps in our health services, as far as finances would permit, starting with the maternity service, and proceeding on through the child welfare clinics, nursery schools and classes, and elementary schools, finally closing the 14 to 16 gap ... [with] the whole nation being brought under medical care and attention of some sort from birth upwards ... all [members of the Committee] considered that the general conception was admirable and steps should be taken to work it out in detail'[42], after Chamberlain, the great social reformer, had given expression to some of his deepest feelings.

While fervently supporting Chamberlain's vision of comprehensive national health services in a memo. urging a bold 'national health policy for the next election', Ball also sought to foster the Committee's interest in 'harnessing the present day urge for games and physical recreation for Party purposes ... not by interfering with the Junior Imperial League [then the Party's youth wing] or with other existing Conservative organisations, but by getting up an entirely new body with an executive and council composed of prominent athletes, social workers and other people of sound political views ... the activities of any such organisation could be translated into votes at the next election'.[43] In studying the possibilities for constructing such a scheme, the Department examined the experience of Italy, Germany and Czechoslovakia.

The 1935 election manifesto, drafted by the indefatigable Brooke on the basis of the Committee's conclusions, contained a vigorous call for 'a great combined effort … to raise still further the general health of the Nation' and, despite the heavy costs of rearmament foreshadowed in 1935, Chamberlain found some money to advance his vision a little with the establishment in 1936 of a national service of midwives. He also took up the issue of the national physique in a number of speeches in the late 1930s with a fervour that suggests that he shared Ball's view that minds in healthier bodies would be more inclined to vote Tory. The press applauded his efforts to an extent that 'amazed' Ball.[44] By 1937 the two men were considering a scheme for a National College of Physical Training with grants to assist its pupils, and advisory fitness councils to spread public enthusiasm.[45] Underlying all this effort, which finally achieved a little success with the extension of training and the provision of national recreation camps in 1938, there was 'a wish to draw on the enthusiasm for fitness that the Fascists were exploiting and to guide it into safer political channels' to the Party's advantage.[46] Could there also have been a feeling that weedy Englishmen might not be much of a match for hunky Germans if conflict should break out?

What Ball and the rest of the private army relished was the extension of research work into new areas following the launch of Chamberlain's plans for a fresh programme of government. Assignments included 'the general outlook for world trade', 'keeping progress notes of Roosevelt's efforts in the U.S.A.', and approaching 'the German Ministry of Labour for details of work-sharing schemes'.[47] Disappointments were inevitable. Nothing came of a number of the initial ideas that Chamberlain and Ball had drawn up in 1934. That is the way of political research. No one ever managed to find a means of overcoming the deep-seated problems of British agriculture despite hours of research devoted to them by the Department. But some notable successes occurred. There was a great sense of satisfaction, which was widely shared, with the outcome of work, commissioned by Chamberlain, on 'the relations which should exist in future between the State and Industry' embodied in a report completed in October 1934.

> The essential character of the proposals was that Government should come into the industry, secure a reconstruction that was acceptable to employers and workers, and then leave the industry to carry on with its work. This was exemplified in the strict provision that reorganisation schemes should not be a barrier to new firms coming into the industry or inhibit other such developments in the future. This approach underlay much that the Baldwin and Chamberlain Governments did before 1939, especially in the coal and cotton industries, but it also came remarkably close to the policy that emerged from the Industrial Policy Committee after 1945.[48]

Indeed, this was only one area in which there was considerable continuity between Neville Chamberlain's and Rab Butler's Research Departments. It seemed prudent after 1945 to emphasise how much the Party had changed since the days that had been tarnished so severely by appeasement. In reality Butler was very much Chamberlain's political heir. The admiration was unqualified. Butler wrote in 1941 that he 'thought Neville was like Saul in one respect and the younger Pitt in another. He was like Saul because he towered head and shoulders above all other members of the Cabinet, and like the younger Pitt because he was definitely a man of peace and a husbander of the nation's resources'.[49] The two men both believed that Conservatives should not hesitate to use the power of the state if it was needed to secure economic and social progress.

The extent of the continuity would have been absolutely obvious if Chamberlain, who became Prime Minster in 1937, had fought the election which he planned for 1939 or 1940. David Clarke, who was to run the Research Department after 1945, was put in charge of planning the manifesto. He proposed to include 'a national scheme of family allowances on a contributory basis', 'the extension of medical benefits to the wives and children of those insured under the existing National Health Scheme', 'a general increase of pensions to existing pensioners with low incomes', the introduction of technical schools and nursery schools where they were needed, the extension of social insurance to non-manual workers earning less than £250 a year, an enhanced 'National Fitness Campaign', and 'the establishment of some new national body for advising industrialists on the siting of new factories'. Ideally, Clarke said, the aims should be even bolder, in conformity with Chamberlain's life-time commitment to social improvement. But that depended on a peaceful settlement of the European crisis which, in Clarke's words, 'would radically alter the whole financial outlook for the future. It would then be possible to look forward to higher expenditure upon the extension of the social services than can safely be contemplated with the present burden of armaments'.[50] Chamberlain's desperate search for peace was intimately linked with his continuing ambition 'to elevate the condition of the people' – his all-consuming passion in politics. If peace had by some miracle been preserved, there is every reason to suppose that an election would have produced a thumping majority for Chamberlain's evolving Tory welfare state and killed off socialism in Britain. If that had happened, the remarkable little army in Old Queen Street under the brilliant, amoral Ball would have gained the kind of recognition that Butler's much larger Research Department was to secure after 1945.

*

In the dramatic Commons debates of May 1940 which brought Chamberlain's premiership to an end, Henry Brooke, who had become MP for Lewisham West in 1938, spoke up strongly for the chief whom he admired so much. As Chamberlain lay dying five months later, Joseph Ball wrote to him proposing that they mount a vigorous campaign in defence of his record. But it was of course too late. Cancer forced Chamberlain to resign as a Cabinet Minster and as Leader of the Conservative Party in October 1940. When he died the following month, he held just one post: the Chairmanship of the Conservative Research Department.

Some fifty years later when I was moving the battered, but handsome leather-topped desk used by Directors of the Department, what looked like a faded, dusty old pamphlet fell out. It was the

Order of Service for Chamberlain's funeral in Westminster Abbey on 14 November 1940, complete with instructions about what to do in the event of an air raid. Perhaps Ball had returned to Old Queen Street after the service and pushed it absent-mindedly between the drawers of the desk. However it got there, it seemed appropriate that the sad little memento of this great, tragic man should have survived at the centre of the Department which mattered so much to him.

Notes

The essential introduction to the history of the Conservative Party in this period is John Ramsden, *The Age of Balfour and Baldwin 1902-1940* (Longman, 1978). The same impeccable scholarship distinguishes his history of the Conservative Research Department up to 1979, *The Making of Conservative Party Policy*, which followed two years later (Longman, 1980). This chapter draws heavily on it.

I am grateful to Jeremy McIlwaine, the Conservative Party's Archivist at the Bodleian Library, for looking after me so well when I worked on the CRD records at the end of last year. I am grateful too for some interesting points sent to me by Henry Brooke's son, Peter, now Lord Brooke of Sutton Mandeville. I also acknowledge the kind help of Alexandra Herdman in preparing this chapter.

Published sources are cited in full on first mention: thereafter short titles are used.

[1] For details, see Scott Kelly, '"The Ghost of Neville Chamberlain": Guilty Men and the 1945 Election' in *Conservative History Journal*, Autumn 2005, pp 18–24.

[2] David Faber, *Munich: The 1938 Appeasement Crisis* (Simon & Schuster, 2008). My review of this outstanding book can be found on the blue blog section of the Conservative Party's website.

[3] Quoted in Robert Self, *Neville Chamberlain: A Biography* (Ashgate Publishing Limited, 2006), p. 105. This is by far the best single volume biography of Chamberlain, based on a very wide range of published and unpublished sources.

[4] For a summary of its principal achievements, see my *Party of Change: A Brief History of the Conservatives* (Conservative Research Department, 2008), pp 19–20.

[5] Quoted in Self, *Chamberlain*, p. 439.

[6] Ibid.

7. Ibid., p. 5.
8. John Ramsden, *The Making of Conservative Party Policy: The Conservative Research Department since 1929* (Longman, 1980), pp 23–4.
9. Ibid., p. 25.
10. Ibid., p. 28.
11. R. R. James (ed.), *Memoirs of a Conservative: J. C. C. Davidson's Memoirs and Papers 1910–37* (Weidenfeld and Nicolson, 1969), p. 275.
12. Ramsden, *Making of Conservative Party Policy*, p. 33.
13. Lord Percy of Newcastle, *Some Memories* (Eyre & Spottiswoode, 1958), p. 149.
14. Thomas Jones, *Whitehall Diary: Volume II 1926/1930*, (ed.) Keith Middlemas (Oxford University Press, 1969), p. 229.
15. Ramsden, *Making of Conservative Party Policy*, p. 42.
16. *Memoirs of a Conservative*, p. 272.
17. For a glimpse of Ball's dark deeds in support of appeasement, see Faber, *Munich*, pp 85–90.
18. 'Memorandum for the Director', September 1930, Conservative Research Department Papers, CRD 1/12/1, Conservative Party Archive, Bodleian Library, Oxford.
19. Ibid.
20. Ball to Marjorie Maxse (copy), 24 February 1932, Conservative Research Department Papers, ibid.
21. Chamberlain to Ball, 27 February 1933, Conservative Research Department Papers, CRD 1/14/7.
22. Self, *Chamberlain*, p. 221.
23. Peter Brooke's words in a letter to the author, 20 April 2009, referring to these articles 'which I am convinced were written by my father'.
24. Ramsden, *Making of Conservative Party Policy*, p. 43.
25. Frank Longford, *Eleven at No. 10: A Personal View of Prime Ministers* (Harrap, 1984), pp 35–6.
26. 'Copy of Confidential Minute from Mr Ball to Mr Lloyd, 3rd February 1931', Conservative Research Department Papers, CRD 1/8/1.
27. Conservative Research Department Papers, CRD 1/2/11.
28. Ramsden, *Making of Conservative Party Policy*, p. 53.
29. Ibid. For further details of the Committee's work, see J. A. Cross, *Lord Swinton* (Clarendon Press,1982), pp 96–7.
30. Conservative Research Department Papers, CRD 1/9/5.
31. Hoare to Ball, 3 May 1932, Conservative Research Department Papers, CRD 1/54/3.
32. Graham Stewart, *Burying Caesar: Churchill, Chamberlain and the Battle for the Tory Party* (Weidenfeld and Nicolson, 1999), p. 123.

[33] Ball to Butler (copy), 2 November 1936, Conservative Research Department Papers, CRD 1/54/4.
[34] Clarke memo. to Ball, 8 March 1938, Conservative Research Department Papers, CRD 1/54/4.
[35] Viscount Mersey's Diary, 6 July 1939, printed in his *A Picture of Life 1872–1940* (John Murray, 1941), p. 426.
[36] For details, see Ramsden, *Making of Conservative Party Policy*, pp 46–51.
[37] Ibid., pp 72–5.
[38] Ibid., p. 77.
[39] 'Notes of Discussion with the Chancellor of the Exchequer 30/1/34', Conservative Research Department Papers, CRD 1/64/1.
[40] Ramsden, *Making of Conservative Party Policy*, p. 78.
[41] 'Conservative Consultative [sic] Committee Index and Summary', Conservative Research Department Papers, CRD 1/64/13.
[42] 'C. C. C. Notes of Meetings', 6 July 1934, Conservative Research Department Papers, CRD 1/64/2.
[43] Ball to Chamberlain (copy), 13 July 1934, Conservative Research Department Papers, CRD 1/64/1.
[44] Ball to Chamberlain (copy), 12 October 1936, Conservative Research Department Papers, CRD 1/24/2.
[45] Conservative Research Department Papers, CRD 1/24/3.
[46] Ramsden, *Making of Conservative Party Policy*, p. 83.
[47] Conservative Research Department Papers, CRD 1/64/13.
[48] Ramsden, *Making of Conservative Party Policy*, p. 82.
[49] Butler to Lord Dunglass, the future Lord Home, (copy), 8 October 1941, Conservative Research Department Papers, CRD 2/53/1.
[50] Conservative Research Department Papers, CRD 1/7/37.

Alistair Cooke and Stephen Parkinson
RAB BUTLER'S GOLDEN ERA?

ALISTAIR COOKE, the editor of this volume, also contributed the first essay where his biographical note appears. STEPHEN PARKINSON joined CRD in 2004 from Cambridge where, like Rab Butler, he was President of the Union. He worked first on the Home Office desk and then in the Political Section. After a year as Director of Research at the Centre for Policy Studies, he returned to Conservative Campaign Headquarters as a member of the Party's target seats campaign, and is the Parliamentary candidate for Newcastle upon Tyne North. His first book, Arena of Ambition: A History of the Cambridge Union, *was published earlier this year.*

> The two arguments used by those who have not yet changed [their allegiance to Labour] are: 1) The Conservatives were responsible for the millions of unemployed in the years 1928/1936; 2) The Conservatives have no policy of social reform and help for the working classes
>
> (H. Cobden Turner, in a letter written from Peel Works, Silk Street, Salford, to Winston Churchill, 5 November 1947, Conservative Research Department Papers, CRD 2/27/1, Conservative Party Archive, Bodleian Library, Oxford).

Churchill's correspondent was a man of discernment. His letter pinpointed the predicament faced by the Tories after their crushing defeat at the 1945 general election which gave Labour an overall Parliamentary majority of 146. Disillusionment with the Attlee government's conduct of national affairs, the absence of any semblance of sustained economic revival and the miseries caused by harsh winters, brought the Tories some modest revival of their fortunes within a couple of years, with clear evidence of growing support in places in and around Manchester which had swung heavily to Labour in 1945. But there could be no prospect of election victory until the two great charges against them, of which Mr Cobden Turner now reminded Churchill, had been effectively answered. Naturally the Tories marshalled historical fact in their defence. Unemployment had risen sharply to nearly three million during the Labour government of 1929–31. No leader of the Party had ever taken a greater interest in social reform than Neville Chamberlain, under whose government a thousand new homes had been built every day. But in 1947 such facts were not much help. In a Britain where Labour had established such a powerful political ascendancy (assisted by Churchill's disastrous 'Gestapo' election broadcast in 1945), the Tories were condemned as upper-class, out of touch and uncompassionate – the Party of two nations, not one.

In the Labour-dominated post-war world, whose gods were Beveridge and Keynes, the Conservatives had much urgent work to do in order to re-establish themselves as a potential Party of government. Humility and penitence were rightly the order of the day. As Iain Macleod, one of the famous products of the post-war CRD, was to put it several years later:

> It would have been impossible for the Conservative Party, after its defeat in 1945, to reform and reorganise itself if it had contemptuously said that the electors had chosen wrongly. Instead we started from the assumption that it was we, the Conservative Party, who were at fault and not the people of this country.[1]

However, not everyone saw things quite that way. The wake-up call from Salford did not stir Churchill's office into action to hasten the progress of reform and reorganisation. The Tory leader was preoccupied with writing his magisterial, if highly tendentious, war memoirs, on which his own future financial security depended, and with developing profound reflections on international affairs which he embodied in momentous speeches delivered abroad. The Salford letter was sent round to the Conservative Research Department, now re-installed in its old home at 24 Old Queen Street (and enlarged by the acquisition of a kind of annexe at number 34 on a seven-year lease, subsequently extended until 1979). The Department had been badly run down during the war: like many other offices, it was closed in early 1940, and its furniture put into storage. Thanks to David Clarke and Henry Brooke, two linchpins of the Chamberlain era, there were some stirrings of life towards the end of the war – but at the time of the 1945 general election, the Department remained a 'ghost ship',[2] consisting only of the two men and two secretaries.[3]

If Churchill had had his way, the post-war CRD would not have amounted to very much. He wanted to recreate it as no more than a little support staff for himself and his ex-ministerial colleagues under his brusque, unintellectual son-in-law, Duncan Sandys, who had lost his seat at the general election. This prospect appalled many in the Conservative hierarchy – not least Sir Joseph Ball, the pre-war Director of CRD, who had taken the Department's records into his custody for safe-keeping – and Churchill was forced to abandon the plan. The form in which CRD was actually revived meant that it swiftly acquired an extensive role – far wider than it had had before 1939 – with a dominant ethos that was finely tuned to the Party's overriding need to tackle the severe problems that the Salford letter had highlighted. Indeed, by November 1947 when the letter reached Old Queen Street, the Department had just come to the end of the first stage of its post-war policy work. It had made possible the successful completion and launch of the document which presented Conservative policy in a form suited to the fundamental requirements of the time – the instantly famous *Industrial Charter* which the Party approved at its 1947 Conference in Brighton. That set the scene for further policy work, conceived in the same spirit, which culminated in the fullest statement of policy that the Party had so far produced, *The Right Road for Britain*, in 1949. It equipped the Party with the means of dealing with the predicament summed up by the Salford letter.

*

This essential task was successfully accomplished because it was placed in exactly the right hands. From the moment that he became CRD Chairman, everyone agreed that Rab Butler was perfect for the part. Butler came from a family with very strong academic credentials: his mother was a descendant of Adam Smith, and among his paternal line were two Headmasters of Harrow, a Headmaster of Haileybury, and Professors at Oxford, St Andrews and London. At Butler's own university, Cambridge, his great-uncle was (like him) Master of Trinity and his father Master of Pembroke, the College where both he and Rab studied as undergraduates. Rab lived up to the high familial standard, taking a Double First in Modern Languages and History and being elected to a Fellowship at Corpus Christi, where he lectured and supervised undergraduates. These credentials made him, in John Ramsden's words, 'a brilliantly successful choice' for CRD:

> Butler's background ... gave him an understanding of the processes of research that was available to few of his senior contemporaries, and a recognition of the necessary tolerance that would be required if very bright minds were to be used effectively in the Party's service. He also had by 1946 sufficient weight and experience in the higher reaches of the Party to protect his protégés from a suspicious Central Office, which under [Lord] Woolton [as Party Chairman] was unhappy about having to pay the Research Department's bills* without controlling its activities in any way.[4]

---

* The bills amounted to nearly £60,000 in 1949 (around £1.6 million in today's values), slightly less in the 1950s when the Party was in power. CRD had 'a certain income of its own from invested funds' at this time, nearly all of which was passed by the Party's Treasurers annually (memo. by David Clarke, 3 August 1951 and note on CRD budget, September 1957, Conservative Research Department Papers, CRD 2/53/5). In 1946 the lease on 24 Old Queen Street from Christ's Hospital, which owned the freehold, had 'about 40 years to run ... the whole house was considered by architects before the war to be in rather a poor condition' (Michael Fraser to a Miss Martin (copy), 13 September 1946, CRD 2/53/57). The garden was 'rented reputedly from the Ministry of Works', according to Clarke's memo., 3 August 1951.

To Butler went the credit for success. Even Harold Macmillan, who was not always conspicuous in the ranks of his admirers, lauded him for his CRD achievements:

> Inside the Party and in academic and intellectual circles, Butler managed matters with extraordinary skill. Backed by the highly gifted members of the Research Department, he had been largely responsible for the development of the new policy. He defended it with equal knowledge and subtlety.[5]

No one in those post-war years of policy reformulation referred to Butler without mentioning the Research Department in the same breath. It was his domain and he showed a deep, affectionate interest in all that happened in it – something that Chamberlain, who had valued it just as greatly, had never managed to display. The day that the Department moved back into Old Queen Street after the war from temporary premises elsewhere, Butler wrote to David Clarke, its very experienced first post-war Director. 'Dear David', his letter of 29 August 1946 ran, 'I write to welcome you all to your office at 24 Old Queen Street, where I shall look forward to joining you in October. Please wish everybody all the best. I shall hope to get to know them in the autumn when I have a proper office of my own. Yrs ever, Rab'. Clarke replied on 3 September: 'Dear Rab, It was a very kind thought of yours to write and welcome us to our new offices. We look forward to having our Chairman with us again for the first time for fifteen years [Chamberlain having been briefly in residence before returning to government in 1931]. The only advantage of the Party being in opposition seems to be that the Chairman of the Research Department has his office with us instead of some Government Department. Yours ever, David'.[6]

It was the beginning of a warm two-way relationship in which members of the Department felt involved as the staff grew to some fifty by the time of the 1950 general election, about half of them being secretaries who were in the charge of the formidable Avis Lewis. 'Avis was the only one who scared us all,' one of Clarke's successors as Director recalled.[7] But she is said to have looked very sympathetically on the most celebrated of all CRD romances, which united Enoch Powell with his secretary, Pamela Wilson. Avis Lewis decided 'that Miss Wilson was the secretary who might be able to persuade Brigadier Powell to smile'.[8] And so she did – to the lasting happiness of both of them. (In CRD folklore the story acquired some remarkable embellishments – with the courtship being transferred to the privacy of a CRD cupboard – which intrigued the impressionable young Ferdinand Mount when he joined the Department some fifteen years later.[9])

Apart from the fear sometimes inspired by Avis Lewis (who was to have some feared, but also much-loved, successors), those who worked in the Department during this important creative period must have seen it as a most agreeable diarchy. Butler and Clarke ran it in perfect harmony: and Chairman and Director continued to find themselves in total accord after Clarke, in search of a different kind of research work, left just before the 1951 election to be replaced by his own first post-war CRD recruit, Michael Fraser, known to everyone as Mike in his pre-CRD days, improbable though that would have seemed to those who encountered him in his later years of greatness.* (After a reconstruction of the Department in 1948, there were two other joint Directors, Henry Hopkinson and Percy Cohen, but they were not involved in the central issues of policy.) To Clarke belongs much of the glory. He was that *rara avis*, an unsung hero who was content to remain unsung. His *Times* obituarist concluded: 'Whereas his successor at the Research Department, Lord Fraser of Kilmorack, was laden with honours, Clarke, a true intellectual, was content to pass his life in ruminative obscurity'.[10] Though he may have been virtually unknown, the Conservative post-war revival owed just about as much to him as it did to Butler.

That was partly because of his great skill in recruitment. It was Clarke, rather than Butler, who gathered together the CRD's post-war team. Not all those who felt called to CRD's service were chosen; Ted Heath, who saw that the 'CRD was evidently the place

---

*Ted Heath, who became a friend of Fraser during the war, wrote to him as 'My dear Mike' in June 1948, signing himself 'Teddy', the style he used in early life (Conservative Research Department papers, CRD 2/6/9(1).)

for ambitious young men',[11] was disappointed (perhaps his political career would have proceeded more gloriously if he had had the benefit of a CRD training and its engaging camaraderie). Clarke's team did of course include the famous three – Reginald Maudling, Enoch Powell and Iain Macleod – whose very presence has contributed greatly to the impression that this was CRD's golden era: 'There is perhaps no time in the Research Department's history that has been so much reminisced about as the years when Maudling, Powell and Macleod worked there'.[12] Butler himself readily accepted, as a note in the Research Department's papers makes clear, that he did not furnish CRD 'with a hand-picked Brains Trust'. The 'so-called Butler Boys' were unknown to him 'before they joined'.[13] Maudling arrived first in November 1945 while things were still in some confusion. Powell presented himself for interview with Clarke in early 1946 in full Brigadier's uniform. Macleod followed shortly afterwards in 'more conversational and relaxed' fashion.[14]

Because they later became so famous, Maudling, Powell and Macleod's work as backroom boys has been invested with undue significance. Until November 1948 their backroom was not even, strictly speaking, a part of the Research Department, but of the allied Conservative Parliamentary Secretariat, established to provide a briefing and drafting service for ex-ministers who had suddenly been deprived of civil servants by an unexpected election defeat and for backbench MPs, half of whom had never sat in Parliament before. 'Clarke was never to forget the experience of vetting an immaculately dressed Brigadier for a job that largely involved taking minutes at committee meetings and preparing briefs for debates and speeches'.[15]

The famous trio were rushed off their feet helping the Parliamentary Party in 1947–8 when staff numbers were still small. 'Powell prepared about forty briefing notes on the legislation [Labour's Town and Country Planning Bill] between January and August 1947, including a thirty-seven page summary of proceedings at the committee stage, in addition to his briefings for debates on house-building, rural housing and local government finance, among others, during the same period'.[16] He was also responsible for all defence matters, convinced already that the United States was

Britain's real adversary in the post-war world. Macleod was equally busy. By the summer of 1947 'he was handling in addition to Scottish affairs and health, labour, social services, Home Office issues, welfare and local government, while his assistant, Miss Rose, was helping with insurance and pensions'.[17] Even Maudling, the least diligent of the three, managed sixty-four briefings on fuel and power in 1947, an output which his impressionable biographer regards as 'astonishing'.[18]

Largely unbidden, Powell produced an extraordinary 25,000-word policy paper in 1946 calling for an extremely costly new commitment to India (with the state reorganising the whole of industry and agriculture) at the very moment when the Attlee government was preparing to scuttle.[19] In Butler's pithy summary, Powell's thesis was 'that with ten divisions we could reconquer India', but he agreed to submit the paper to Churchill, 'who seemed distressed and asked me if I thought Powell was "all right". I said I was sure he was, but explained that he was very determined in these matters.'[20]

However, the famous three had no real opportunity to contribute much to the vital Butler/Clarke policy-making operation, for which a separate group had been assembled in 1946 in CRD itself, until the Parliamentary Secretariat was merged with the Research Department at the end of 1948. Powell departed the following year following his selection as a Parliamentary candidate: and Maudling and Macleod joined him in the House of Commons in February 1950. Macleod left his mark on *The Right Road for Britain* in 1949 which committed the Tories firmly to the maintenance of the NHS and the post-war social security system, but his policy proposals for Scotland in Butler's series of policy Charters found little favour. Powell devised a policy for Wales, advocating state action to secure economic revival (a much less ambitious version of his prescription for India at marked variance with his subsequent philosophy), which became another Charter in 1949: only a small part of it was actually implemented when the Party returned to power. Maudling perhaps made the greatest contribution to policy. Throughout his four years in the backrooms he operated as a kind of one-man economic advisory council, contributing to the *Industrial Charter*, to Anthony Eden's campaign popularising the concept of the property-owning democracy and to all Churchill's main economic pronouncements, though he found the great man's 'attitude to economic problems was a fairly cavalier one. These things, he felt, should take care of themselves' – 'and who is to say', the clever but rather indolent Maudling added characteristically, 'that he was wrong?'[21]

What Maudling, Macleod and Powell got from the Research Department was an excellent all-round training in politics in much the same manner as other able, ambitious people who were to pass through it over the years. Rather than standing out as unusual or untypical, their work illustrates in a particularly striking fashion CRD's role in sustaining the Party in opposition and in helping to prepare it for government in this period. They were not the first CRD graduates to enter Parliament: Henry Brooke, the unsuccessful future Home Secretary, had gone before. They did not form a special charmed circle around Butler, whom they never got to know particularly well. Their work was reviewed by Clarke, who sometimes insisted on significant revisions, telling Macleod for example to redo some of his briefing on pensions issues in 1946–7.[22]

Clarke knew how to get work successfully completed to a high standard with minimal fuss, as the young Brendon Sewill discovered:

> In July-August 1951, as a young undergraduate doing a vacation job (now called work experience) at CRD, I was set to study the effect on the cost of living of removing the food subsidies (essential if food rationing was to be brought to an end). After a month of studying the subject I served up my paper to David Clarke. After reading it while I sat there, he took his pipe out of his mouth and said 'you've forgotten the marginal elasticity of demand.' So I went back for another month to revise the paper, and thereafter remained impressed with the academic rigour demanded by the Department.[23]

After Clarke's departure in 1951, Butler established his own personal triumvirate at the top with Michael Fraser, 'the best adjutant the Party has ever had'[24] who, like all successful adjutants, had few strong ideas of his own, and the outstandingly able Peter Goldman, the one individual personally appointed to CRD by Butler. In his memoirs Butler said of Goldman that his 'loss to the Party would later be as important as the resignation of any Cabinet Minister'.[25] That could not have been a huge comfort to Goldman who had wanted to be a Cabinet Minister, not a permanent backroom boy. Though Butler was forever writing letters on his behalf, constituencies just did not take to this aloof, rather arrogant man. In his fulsome missives, now in the Butler Papers at Trinity College, Cambridge, his patron kept asking constituencies not to hold Goldman's Jewish background against him. When his chance finally came, it destroyed him: he was the candidate at the most disastrous by-election of the period, at Orpington in 1962, where a Tory majority of nearly 15,000 was replaced by a Liberal majority of almost 8,000.

It was a tragic end to one of the most significant of all CRD backroom careers – a career from which Butler in particular profited enormously. Butler's great verbal felicity and subtlety did not really extend to paper. Goldman drafted quickly and with the utmost elegance. Their association was seen at its finest in Butler's memoirs, *The Art of the Possible*, which Goldman largely wrote for him. They are, as all reviewers agreed, in a class of their own. A further volume, *The Art of Memory*, which Butler produced unassisted, is in a distinctly inferior category. Perhaps Goldman would have made a first-rate Cabinet Minister; he could hardly have proved more valuable, as Butler so readily acknowledged (in words that were his own), than in the job he actually did until his Orpington catastrophe. Whether in CRD itself or in the allied Conservative Political Centre (CPC) which he directed for some years, Goldman crafted text after text following Clarke's departure in 1951, as the Tories prepared for further periods in government in 1955 and 1959. He also wrote a useful biography of Neville Chamberlain, CRD's founder, for Iain Macleod to publish, stressing Chamberlain's commitment to developing the nation's health services which Macleod himself had inherited.

Other high-fliers followed the famous three 'Butler boys', as they were misleadingly dubbed, into Parliament, while those who stayed in the Department, some for their entire careers, invariably won the respect, and often the affection, of successive generations of frontbenchers for whom they toiled and drafted. The desk officers did not form an exclusive male preserve. A number of women forged successful careers in the Department. Diana Spearman was a prominent figure in the economics section for a number of years. Elizabeth Briggs (now Buchanan) worked closely with Douglas Hurd's father, Anthony, one of the Party's leading authorities on agriculture, which was then of decisive importance in many seats. (Over thirty years later her daughter, another Elizabeth, was to follow in her footsteps at the start of her career, later becoming Deputy Private Secretary to the Prince of Wales.) Ursula Branston joined the Parliamentary Secretariat from the BBC in 1946 and became head of the CRD's foreign affairs section in the 1950s. She fondly recalled the 'unorthodox, but ideal conditions' in 34 Old Queen Street: 'An eccentric, push-button, brass and mahogany lift – supreme comfort for one, hell for two' – took her to 'a large and lofty room' on the top floor with a coal fire. Although the furnishings were 'austere', the windows 'looked out on an unfailingly lovely prospect of St. James's Park' and – most likely of all to stir the envy of today's CRD – 'a cheerful tea-lady brought refreshment' twice a day.[26] She needed a little cheering when, in her early days, the notoriously short-tempered Eden threw a book at her. He sent her slightly stronger refreshment – a case of sherry – by way of apology.

CRD flourished after 1951 with Fraser acquiring increasing dominance within it as Butler became a steadily more remote figure, absorbed in the business of government, at which he excelled.* But he still found time to bring his donnish skills to the Department's work: Sir Peter Tapsell, who worked in CRD for three years after coming down from Oxford in 1954, recalled how even junior desk officers were invited, in groups of three or four, into Butler's office

---

*Footnote overleaf.

for 'the most delightful chats – almost like an Oxford tutorial – in which we would exchange ideas'.[27] CRD's sense of continuity matched that of the Party itself during the long years that it remained in power before the 1964 election ended the era. The Department had earned its firmly established place in the order of things. The work done in its backrooms between 1946 and 1951 had enabled the Party to shape its entire post-war approach to domestic politics.

*

Rab Butler was well-prepared for his years at the helm of the post-war CRD. He entered Parliament (at the age of twenty-six) on the Opposition benches. He became an MP in 1929 – at an election in which the Labour Party greatly increased its representation at Westminster (from 190 to 288 MPs) and formed a minority government. The defeat came as a surprise to the Conservatives. As well as a major internal crisis, it provoked 'a reassessment of the Conservative stance in all important policies'.[28] Indeed, it was for this purpose that the Conservative Research Department was created in that year. Butler took an early interest in the Department and contributed papers and memoranda from the outset – involvement which surely helped to establish him as an obvious candidate to lead the Party's post-war policy deliberations. His early ministerial career – which unfolded entirely under coalition National Governments – involved two stints at the Ministry of Labour (in 1937–8 and 1945), bringing him into closer contact with Labour MPs and workers'

---

*Fraser sat at the right hand of successive leaders as their close and trusted adviser until 1975. Harold Macmillan noted in his diary on 4 May 1956: 'Michael Fraser – the very intelligent head of the Conservative Research Department came at 10. I asked him to get his staff working on next year's Budget ... This should make an interesting exercise' (*The Macmillan Diaries: The Cabinet Years 1950–1957*, ed. Peter Catterall, Macmillan, 2003, p. 556). Heath described him as 'an intelligent and thoughtful man, but also a very practical one. He was fun to be with because he had an enormous zest for life which included a passion for music' (Edward Heath, *The Course of My Life*, Coronet Books, 1999, pp 115–6). When Fraser retired in 1975, Rab Butler wrote a much-quoted letter regretting that he could not attend a dinner to mark the event. 'There is no one I would rather attend a farewell meeting for than Michael' – a remark widely regarded as a quintessential 'Rabism' (Anthony Howard, *Rab: The Life of R. A. Butler*, Jonathan Cape, 1987, p. 369).

representatives than most of his colleagues. This experience perhaps strengthened his opinion – which he was alone among the Cabinet in expressing [29] – that the Conservatives would lose the 1945 general election. When he was proved correct, Butler immediately understood the scale of the challenge ahead.

Speaking after the Conservatives were firmly back in government in 1956, Butler explained that his aim had been to delineate 'a living and spiritual philosophy' in which to set modern Conservatism, providing it with 'the inspiration necessary to prevail'.[30] The importance of doing this was clear to him long before the 1945 defeat. As a young man, Butler had been much influenced by his uncle, the academic and politician Sir Geoffrey Butler. In *The Tory Tradition*, a series of lectures he delivered at the University of Pennsylvania in 1914, Sir Geoffrey stressed the importance of rooting Conservative thinking in its history. 'The captains of Toryism in the past can be made the instructors of Toryism in the present,' he explained: 'and the Tory tradition is the Tory hope'.[31] When Tory hopes were shaken after 1945, Butler reprinted his uncle's lectures with an introduction of his own. 'This tradition at its best', he wrote, 'is responsive to the demands of each new age, empirical as to method, resourceful in expressing itself in popular idiom'.[32]

In 1937, Butler had written to a friend and colleague about the need for a single, clear text outlining Conservative philosophy – in his words, a sort of 'Koran of the Party' or a 'Baedecker of Conservatism'.[33] In the wilderness of Opposition, Butler saw this need as all the more pressing: he commissioned David Clarke's *The Conservative Faith in the Modern Age*, an eloquent and incisive work, published in April 1947. He also persuaded Quintin Hogg to write *The Case for Conservatism* for Penguin (1947). As Butler explained: 'These books were written at an early stage under the aegis of the Research Department so as to restore the whole faith and philosophy of the Conservative Party'.[34]

Neither book contained policy proposals: the purpose was to show how contemporary ideas could fit within the traditions of the Conservative Party. The exercise had to be 'impressionistic' –

painting a picture with broad strokes of the brush rather than providing a series of detailed images.[35] As well as being the right way to repackage Conservative philosophy for an electorate which had just rejected the Party so decisively, this had the advantage of being acceptable to a leader famously disinclined to draw up detailed policy in opposition. But Churchill's reticence was tested by a strong demand from the Party at large, which spilled onto the floor of the 1946 Party Conference at Blackpool. Party members passed a resolution demanding a statement 'setting forth the policy for which the Conservative Party stands'.[36]

What they got was the *Industrial Charter*. Although the preamble to this landmark document paid obeisance to the grass-roots demands and claimed it had been 'drawn up by a Committee appointed as a result of a resolution moved at the Blackpool Conference', it was actually another impressionistic document based on earlier work done by the Research Department. Industrial policy was one of the first two areas selected by Butler when it started to consider future policy in the summer of 1946 (the other was taxation) – but this did not guarantee that the work would fall to CRD.[37] Indeed, Churchill set up a separate Industrial Policy Committee in response to the Blackpool resolution rather than refer the matter straight to the Research Department. Was this a snub, or was the decision to establish a broad-based Committee an attempt to include a cross-section of the Parliamentary Party and to respond to the Conference resolution? Either way, Churchill named Butler as Chairman, the Committee met in Butler's office at Old Queen Street, and it was served by CRD staff (Clarke was its Secretary, assisted by Maudling and Fraser). The choice of Butler was a striking compliment given the Committee's powerful composition: it contained three future Chancellors of the Exchequer (Butler, Macmillan and Derick Heathcoat-Amory), the incumbent Shadow Chancellor (Oliver Stanley), and a future Lord Chancellor (David Maxwell Fyfe). Butler chaired it adroitly, producing a report not only with no dissentients but 'with Butler's hand clearly revealed in the wording'.[38]

The *Industrial Charter* was published on 12 May 1947. In producing it, Butler consciously followed the example set by Sir Robert Peel's *Tamworth Manifesto* more than a century earlier. The two documents shared the same objective: a transformation of the public image of the Conservative Party at one decisive stroke. 'As in the days of Peel', Butler wrote later, the Conservatives needed to 'be seen to have accommodated themselves to a social revolution'.[39] Peel knew that the Conservative Party which he had founded would not win elections while it was widely, if unfairly, perceived to be opposed to political reform. Tamworth committed it in strong, though largely general, terms to moderate, progressive change. Butler's *Industrial Charter* demonstrated equally emphatically that there was no truth whatsoever in the widespread view, so carefully fostered by their opponents, that the Conservatives were irredeemably the Party of high unemployment and would not lift a finger to help those in hardship.

True to the spirit of Peel, the *Industrial Charter* did not spell out what the Tories would actually do in office – but it gave a clear signal that the Party had accepted the key elements of what has come to be known as the post-war settlement. There was an explicit acceptance of Keynesian policies of demand management and full employment. As well as a promise that a Conservative Government would 'free industry from unnecessary controls and restrictions', there was a recognition that parts of the nationalisation programme would not be reversed. A key section was the 'Workers' Charter' outlining the Party's vague but noble wish 'to humanise, not to nationalise' industry. Butler later explained what lay behind the deliberately bland tone of the document: 'We were out-Peeling Peel in giving the Party a painless but permanent facelift: the more unflamboyant the changes, the less likely were the features to sag again'.[40] He was very content with Churchill's description of it as 'a broad statement of policy, to which those opposed to the spread of rigid socialism can now rally'.[41] His critics accused him of 'pink socialism' and his CRD backroom boys were sometimes described as 'pink pansies'. The critics were not numerous. Their call for clear blue water through the adoption of free market policies was overwhelmingly rejected by the

Party Conference. That approach could not possibly have provided a route back to power in the post-war world.

Five further Charters followed the first great one. All were drafted in the Department either by Clarke himself or under his direction. They covered agriculture (June 1948), women's issues (February 1949), 'policy for Wales and Monmouthshire' (March 1949), imperial policy (June 1949) and 'Scottish control of Scottish affairs' (November 1949). It is not at all clear why these subjects, rather than others, were picked out for special Charter treatment. The *Agricultural Charter* had some significance – 'It is worth noting', Michael Fraser wrote in a 1961 review of CRD's post-war policy work, 'that most of the policies and production targets set out in it have been achieved under Conservative Governments since 1951' – but the others attracted a diminishing level of interest.[42] Fraser's verdict on the women's and imperial Charters was not favourable: the former, he judged, 'had a negligible impact' while the latter did not stand the test of time.[43]

Work extended far beyond the Charters, as Fraser made clear in his account of policy-making in these years. It was overseen by the Party's new Advisory Committee on Policy which brought together representatives of the Parliamentary Party and the Party in the country, and normally acted as Butler's loyal ally – not least because he chaired that too. There was hardly a domestic issue which was left untouched. Town and country planning, gas, electricity, the NHS, transport, social services and the problems of elderly people were just some of the most significant. Work on the social services started with a hugely detailed study of all the legislation that had ever been passed on the subject. The paper began: 'The first Poor Law Act, passed in 1601, recognised the obligation of the community to relieve the destitution of people unable to maintain themselves'.[44] Discussion of social issues had, however, to take account of what the country could afford. A paper entitled 'Basic Security for All', dated 30 April 1948, sounded a strong warning note: 'The enormous cost of old age is a salient feature of all our social security schemes … the social services will become less and less self-financing'.[45] Little of this work, however, led to bold, radical policy proposals for the future.

The Department worked within the framework of the post-war settlement.

Butler 'spent much of his time' at the Research Department, and in late 1948 began to supervise the production of a comprehensive, carefully worded, statement of party policy.[46] The Party at large awaited a full statement with mounting impatience, particularly after the failure to regain two seats from Labour at by-elections in Edmonton and Hammersmith South during the winter of 1948–9, perhaps the most depressing moments in the Tories' dismal by-election performance in this Parliament when they were unable to take a single seat off Labour. With clamour growing, and with the election drawing near, Churchill's interest in policy-making was finally awakened. On 1 April, the Shadow Cabinet agreed that a full statement of Conservative policy should be issued. It appeared in July 1949 as *The Right Road for Britain*.

The chief responsibility for the document was given to a specially formed Committee of the Shadow Cabinet chaired by Anthony Eden, firmly identified in these years with the cause of the property-owning democracy. Butler was, however, an important member of this Committee, with David Clarke and Henry Hopkinson serving as its secretaries; and 'though it was not initially entrusted to the Department it was there that most of the work on it was actually done'.[47] Lord Woolton, the Party Chairman with whom Butler never enjoyed good relations, suggested that the document should be drafted by Quintin Hogg. Given Butler's recollection of the tortuous process of writing and rewriting it involved, this may have been a blessing in disguise: 'Churchill took very little interest in the early stages of the Research Department and very little interest in the production of the Charters, but when it came to *The Right Road for Britain*, he took an interest in every line and comma of the document'.[48] Its careful, balanced tone, and lack of detailed commitments, were calculated to please him.

The final, Churchill-sanctioned version was finally published on 23 July 1949 and was followed by 'an intensive campaign of publicity', including speeches by Churchill and Macmillan and a party political broadcast by Eden, 'all of which were drafted or vetted in the Research Department'.[49] Magazine articles were written for Churchill, Butler and Macmillan, summarising the document's main points for a popular audience. But it was not long before *The Right Road* had to be revised and turned into a manifesto for the looming general election. It was drafted and redrafted many times (as manifestos invariably are) by David Clarke with the help of Pam Wilson (the future Mrs Enoch Powell) at the typewriter. On 17 January 1950 she took the text to Churchill at his London home, 28 Hyde Park Gate, where Eden, Butler, Woolton and others gathered to discuss it with the great man. When she left, Churchill handed her coat to her. The garment immediately acquired a special aura. 'I didn't send it to the cleaners for years', she recalls. Further intensive manifesto work followed. Pam Wilson noted in her diary on 20 January, 'WSC rang about 5 times – food subsidies part of Manifesto changed about 5 times'. The final version stated that 'there will be no reduction which might influence the price of food without compensating increases [in income] to those most affected'– but did not spell out the form such increases would take. The manifesto was published, to 'a good press' as Pam Wilson recorded, on 25 January.[50] Looking back on it all now, her chief recollection is 'how hard we worked – and such long hours – but it was such fun'.[51]

Long hours were spent too in the production of *The Campaign Guide* – drafted for the first time entirely within CRD – and then, as now, 'a co-operative venture which drew on almost all the Department's officers'.[52] *Daily Notes* were posted out to candidates and agents throughout the campaign. All these documents made clear that the Party now had plenty of policies – so that it could no longer be accused, as it had been in 1945, of having nothing to offer – but they were carefully presented in a way that would not restrict a Conservative government's freedom of manoeuvre unduly.

Throughout, the principal aim was always to make clear that the Conservatives would amend and improve, not overturn, Labour's post-war dispensation. As in some other periods of opposition, CRD's policy work may have been extensive, but the conclusions tended to be cautious. On the NHS, for example, the 1950 manifesto stated that the Party would 'maintain and improve the Health Service' through 'administrative efficiency and economy and correct priorities'. Similarly most of Labour's nationalisation was accepted: only steel and road haulage would be freed from state ownership. The emphasis was on securing greater efficiency and value for taxpayers' money. Action did not always follow words which foreshadowed it. The 1950 manifesto proposed that British Railways 'should be reorganised into a number of regional systems, each with its own pride of identity and each administered by its own Board of Directors' – a firm commitment which in government was firmly forgotten. There was caution too on taxation: 'We hope to make sufficient economies [in public spending] to start upon reducing indirect taxation'.

Despite all CRD's efforts to make the Party look responsible, in touch and positive again, Labour were returned with a majority of just five seats at the February 1950 election. There was understandable Conservative frustration at such a result: the Party's remarkable comeback from the debacle of 1945, which took many by surprise, had not been enough. Labour's slender Parliamentary majority gave cause for optimism, however, and the Research Department swiftly began a new phase of policy work .This time the aim was to find and exploit a crucial vote-catching issue.

The obvious candidate for CRD's close attention was housing. Grand promises to construct 'homes fit for heroes' (as in 1918) had made this one of Labour's key planks in the late 1940s – and one of their most conspicuous failures in government. The Department studied the issues at length, producing a succession of long policy papers. The main conclusions which emerged were that 'the need to reduce housing costs should be a guiding principle in housing policy', that 'everything should be done to secure economy by improving the efficiency of the building industry', and that 'a more flexible' renting system should be introduced.[53] The work now acquired a much higher importance. Housing was seen plainly as an election-winner.

A post-election survey conducted by the Research Department showed that every single Tory candidate had made housing a main priority in their 1950 election address. An options paper, drawn up by CRD, was put to Butler in June 1950, asking: 'Do we wish to state a numerical target?'[54] The Party hierarchy thought the risks of doing so were too great – but their caution was swept aside by a famous rebellion at the 1950 Party Conference. The setting, once again, was Blackpool. In the course of the housing debate on the second day of the Conference, one delegate mentioned 300,000 new homes a year as a desirable goal for a Conservative house-building programme. Subsequent speakers picked up the figure with mounting enthusiasm. Woolton, on stage, turned to Butler and whispered: '*Could* we build 300,000?' David Clarke was urgently consulted behind the scenes of the Conference and gave his opinion that it would be technically feasible – so Lord Woolton stepped on to the podium and declared 'in beaming surrender: "This is magnificent".'[55] Churchill repeated the figure in his closing speech, calling it a 'target' rather than a pledge, but there was no backing down.

On their return from Blackpool, a CRD group was set to work exploring the feasibility of the Party's new policy. Its report, circulated in March 1951, set out in stark detail the scale of the commitment. It would require a large reallocation of shipping resources and foreign currency to obtain soft wood; a special increase of 9 per cent in the output of the cement industry; almost one million tons of coal; and about 2,000 million bricks. Thanks largely to CRD's detailed preparations, the policy was successfully implemented when the Party returned to government. The Conservative manifesto of 1955 proudly boasted:

> our Party's pledge to build 300,000 houses a year was derided by our opponents as impossible to fulfil. In fact, nearly 350,000 were built last year, and at least as many are likely to be built this year. [56]

There were many misgivings about the huge reallocation of resources, but the Party profited greatly in electoral terms – and much of Britain was rehoused, even if not always to a very high standard. But it was not the issue which many in CRD would have chosen to place at the very centre of Conservative policy, overshadowing so much of their work in other areas.

*

So was this the CRD's golden era? Was its contribution to the post-war Conservative revival the finest thing it has ever done, as many have suggested? It was certainly Rab Butler's own personal golden era, or rather the central part of a ten-year golden era that began with his great 1944 Education Act and lasted until the mid-1950s, culminating in his highly successful term as Chancellor of the Exchequer after 1951. Though some of his colleagues – Eden in particular – were irritated by the extent of the praise lavished upon him, he dominated the whole of the post-war policy-making process, thanks to the work done for him in CRD. The results may not have been as strikingly original as many were encouraged to believe at the time. The work did not represent a sharp break with Conservative inter-war policy. Baldwin and Chamberlain had associated the Party with vigorous and expanding state action: Butler continued their work in an era which seemed very different because Labour for the first time in their history had seized the intellectual initiative and, in the process, created retrospectively a dominant narrative of events since the 1920s which destroyed the Conservative Party's reputation for competence.

In 1945 a thick red mist enveloped politics. Butler more than anyone else thinned it. Michael Fraser, who saw it all at close quarters, always said that without Butler 'the recovery would not have happened in any lasting way … He was the only person at the top level who really put drive and coherence into the policy exercise'.[57] It was done in the terms which trends in contemporary politics, accentuating the role of the state, made necessary, though that risked the charge of 'pink socialism'. Baldwin and Chamberlain, whom Butler admired so much, would have approved. Churchill, who contributed so little to the policy-making process, never gave it much thought and never warmed towards Butler. Churchill's serious stroke in 1953,which occurred while Eden was out of action after major surgery, gave Butler his first, and greatest, chance of acquiring the leadership. He owed Churchill no particular obligation. 'With hindsight Butler himself considered that July 1953 had been his best chance of becoming Prime Minister'.[58] If he had seen it at the time, his golden era could have brought him the golden crown of politics.

As it was, CRD did not help provide Britain with its Prime Minister, but it made possible Butler's swift ascent to a position where he was such a strong contender for it. Without the CRD that David Clarke fashioned for him, Butler would not have been able to complete in just over four years the policy exercise which brought the Tories unmistakably into the age of Beveridge and Keynes, and gave them an election-winning manifesto in 1951. The rapid expansion of its numbers, and the increase in its functions, enabled it to do far more than 'Neville Chamberlain's private army' with the best will in the world had been able to accomplish. The fusion in 1948 of the short-lived Parliamentary Secretariat with the Department inherited from Chamberlain and Joseph Ball created an organization which, in Butler's words, was both immersed 'in the detail and hurly-burly of day-to-day politics' and responsible for 'long-term research coupled with constructive assistance in reformulating Party policy'.[59] That combination gave it the unique character which it has retained ever since. In later generations its members would work just as hard; their contributions to policy-making would be just as vital. But the 1945–51 period has a golden sheen because this was the first time that the fully fledged Department showed what it could do – and what it did helped to set the scene for election victory. More than a thousand briefs were produced by CRD in these years – well over one brief for every day that Parliament sat.[60] Rab Butler caught the spirit of the place perfectly:

> The burden was heavy and the hours worked often preposterously long, but all of us were buoyed up by the excitement of the period and the sure knowledge that what we were doing would be the basis of any future success of the Conservative Party.[61]

It was the spirit that CRD was to recapture again and again as it helped prepare for government in the decades ahead.

It all sounds idyllic, perhaps even too idyllic. Too much contentment and self-satisfaction can distort historical perspective. Accounts of the 1945–51 period, both published and unpublished, read much like school speech day reports, recounting success after success. Over the years Butler and Fraser in particular polished their versions of what happened: the policy papers that were botched, the ideas that no one wanted, the problems that proved too difficult have all been eliminated from the story. What exactly, people asked, did the Conservative Party mean by 'the property-owning democracy' to which Anthony Eden kept referring as he popularised an idea of the inter-war period invented by a forgotten Scottish MP and thinker, Noel Skelton? Did it involve more than an extension of home-ownership, welcome though that was in a Britain where only four out of fourteen million homes were owner-occupied? What about shares for employees in the businesses they made profitable? Should death duties be cut to keep property in family ownership? How could women take their full place among the ranks of the property owners? After a great deal of time devoted to this 'difficult task', discussion petered out inconclusively.[62] CRD did not even favour promoting home-ownership by every possible means. It helped to kill off the proposal that sitting tenants should be given the right to buy their council houses even after it had been 'adopted unanimously in principle at the Brighton Conference' in 1947 and mentioned in *The Right Road for Britain,* following a decision by the Liberal Party to back this policy.[63] Just one sentence was devoted to the property-owning democracy in the 1950 manifesto. Its serious expansion beyond home ownership had to await the arrival of Margaret Thatcher.

Not everything in CRD was golden, or excitingly new, in the period of post-war recovery. Even the much-vaunted *Industrial Charter*, important though it was in presentational terms, did not represent a major new departure in Conservative thought: it incorporated Keynesian policies accepted by Conservatives in the war-time coalition. The 1951 victory itself was extremely narrow. Despite all the progress made during its years in Opposition, the best the Conservative Party could do against an exhausted and divided Labour Government which had run out of money was to sneak into power with an overall majority of 17 (thanks to the Ulster Unionists) and nearly a quarter a million fewer votes than Labour. Even the internal advances the Party made must be seen in context: 'Any organisational recovery after 1945 was bound to look spectacular when compared to the depths to which things had sunk by 1945'.[64] Butler himself sometimes spoke in more restrained terms about the turn-around in Conservative fortunes:

> I think the ultimate success of the Conservative Party in winning the Election in 1951 by only a small majority was largely due to the decay and decline of the Labour Party at that time ... I think that the actual winning of the Election was due just as much to physical causes as to our bright ideas ... I think what the bright intellectual ideas did was to prepare the country for us to come in whereas the actual physical jerk which got us in was due to the defects of our opponents. This is rather important.[65]

For Butler himself, the connection with CRD, like his entire career, ended bleakly. Without consulting him, Central Office put out a press release after the 1964 election announcing the end of his long period as CRD Chairman. For him there was no grand retirement party, no fulsome expression of thanks for all that he had done after 1945. No one yet has discovered how to banish ingratitude from politics.

Notes

The records of the Conservative Research Department in the Conservative Party Archive at the Bodleian Library, Oxford are abundant and diverse for this period. We are extremely grateful to Jeremy McIlwaine, the Party's Archivist, for making available files from this rich collection with his customary kindness and efficiency. The post-war period is also covered at length in John Ramsden's *The Making of Conservative Party Policy: The Conservative Research Department since 1929* (Longman, 1980), on which we have drawn extensively. In addition, we have consulted many other publications in which the work of CRD is discussed, not always accurately. We are indebted to Brendon Sewill for valuable advice and comments on drafts of this essay, although we alone are responsible for its tone and conclusions.

1. Quoted in John Ramsden, 'Winston Churchill and the Conservative Party' in Lord Butler (ed.), *The Conservatives: A History from their Origins to 1965* (George Allen & Unwin, 1977), p. 425.
2. Anthony Howard, *Rab: The Life of R. A. Butler* (Jonathan Cape, 1987), p. 151.
3. John Ramsden, *The Making of Conservative Party Policy: The Conservative Research Department Since 1929* (Longman, 1980), pp 95, 102.
4. John Ramsden, *The Age of Churchill & Eden 1940-1957* (Longman, 1995), p. 145.
5. Harold Macmillan, *Tides of Fortune 1945-1955* (Macmillan, 1969), p. 304.
6. Conservative Research Department Papers, CRD 2/7/59, Conservative Party Archive.
7. Quoted in Patrick Cosgrave, *The Lives of Enoch Powell* (Bodley Head, 1989), p. 102.
8. Ibid., p. 103
9. Ferdinand Mount, *Cold Cream: My Early Life and Other Mistakes* (Bloomsbury, 2008), p. 266. Mount regarded the embellishments as an example 'of Enoch's taste for melodrama, his determination to inject passion into the commonplace run of things'.
10. *The Times*, 2 November 1998.
11. Edward Heath, *The Course of My Life: My Autobiography* (Coronet Books, 1999), p. 116.
12. Ramsden, *The Making of Conservative Party Policy*, p. 120.
13. Undated note in a ring-binder labelled 'Rab 1945-51 Essay', Conservative Research Department Papers, CRD 2/53/1.
14. Robert Shepherd, *Iain Macleod: A Biography* (Hutchinson, 1994), p. 42.
15. Robert Shepherd, *Enoch Powell: A Biography* (Hutchinson, 1996), p. 58.
16. Ibid, p. 66.
17. Shepherd, *Iain Macleod*, p. 46.
18. Lewis Baston, *Reggie: The Life of Reginald Maudling* (Sutton Publishing, 2004), p. 54.
19. For a summary of this amazing document, see Simon Heffer, *Like the Roman: The Life of Enoch Powell* (Weidenfeld & Nicolson, 1998), pp 109-11.
20. Lord Butler, *The Art of the Possible* (Penguin edition, 1973), p. 141. Ramsden says the notion that Powell 'sought to persuade the Party of the possibility of a military reconquest of India is wide of the mark, but there is no doubt that the British withdrawal from India did upset him deeply' (*The Making of Conservative Party Policy*, p. 122).
21. Reginald Maudling, *Memoirs* (Sidgwick & Jackson, 1978), p. 45.
22. Conservative Research Department Papers, CRD 2/30/1.

23. Brendon Sewill to Alistair Cooke, 2 August 2009.
24. Butler, *The Art of the Possible*, p. 142.
25. Ibid.
26. Quoted in Ramsden, *The Making of Conservative Party Policy*, p. 127.
27. Interview with Sir Peter Tapsell MP, 4 November 2003, quoted in Stephen Parkinson, 'R. A. Butler and the Conservative Research Department, 1945–1951' (unpublished University of Cambridge B.A. thesis, 2004), p. 14.
28. Stuart Ball, *Baldwin and the Conservative Party: The Crisis of 1929–1931* (Yale University Press, 1988), pp xi-xii.
29. Oliver Lyttelton (Viscount Chandos), *The Memoirs of Lord Chandos* (Bodley Head, 1962), p. 307.
30. Quoted in Gerald Sparrow, *'R.A.B.', Study of a Statesman: The Career of Baron Butler of Saffron Walden, CH* (Odhams Books, 1965), p. 249.
31. Quoted in Butler, *The Art of the Possible*, p. 28.
32. Quoted by Chris Patten in the inaugural R. A. Butler Memorial Lecture, reprinted as 'R. A. Butler – What We Missed' in Lady Butler (ed.), *A Rabanthology* (Wilton 95, 1995), p. 103.
33. Butler to Michael Knatchbull (5th Baron Brabourne), 5 February 1938 and 22 November 1937, Brabourne Papers, India Office Library, London.
34. CRD file, 'Notes for Lord Butler's Memoirs', quoted in Ramsden, *The Making of Conservative Party Policy*, p. 108.
35. Butler, *The Art of the Possible*, pp 145–6.
36. Quoted in J. D. Hoffman, *The Conservative Party in Opposition, 1945–1951* (MacGibbon & Key, 1964), p. 141.
37. Ramsden, *The Making of Conservative Party Policy*, p. 108.
38. Hoffman, p. 147. Hoffman compares the wording of the *Charter* to the text of a speech Butler made on 30 March 1946 (i.e. predating even the establishment of the Industrial Policy Committee) and finds 'a number of suggestions ... all of which formed an important part of *The Industrial Charter*' (p. 146).
39. Butler, *The Art of the Possible*, p. 135.
40. Ibid., pp 145-6.
41. Quoted in a paper by Butler entitled 'Prelude to Brighton', 31 July 1947, Butler Papers, RAB 6, Conservative Party Archive. (This is a small collection of his personal papers from the Research Department, and quite separate from the main Butler archive at Trinity College, Cambridge.)
42. Michael Fraser, 'The Conservative Research Department and Conservative Recovery after 1945', unpublished paper dated August 1961, Conservative Research Department Papers, CRD 2/53/5.
43. Ibid.
44. Conservative Research Department Papers, CRD 2/27/1.
45. Ibid., CRD 2/29/1.

[46] Hoffman, p. 183.
[47] Ramsden, *The Making of Conservative Party Policy*, p. 135.
[48] Ibid., p. 108.
[49] Ibid., p. 140.
[50] Diary extracts kindly supplied by Mrs Enoch Powell.
[51] Mrs Enoch Powell to Alistair Cooke, 25 November 2004.
[52] Ramsden, *The Making of Conservative Party Policy*, pp 141–3.
[53] Conservative Research Department Papers, CRD 2/23/6.
[54] Ramsden, *The Making of Conservative Party Policy*, p. 157.
[55] Hoffman, p. 202; Butler, *The Art of the Possible*, p. 155.
[56] Iain Dale (ed.), *Conservative Party General Election Manifestos, 1900–1997* (Routledge, 2000), p. 119. Alistair Cooke contributed an introductory essay to this book in which he reviews critically the composition and character of Conservative manifestos.
[57] Quoted in Ramsden, 'Winston Churchill and the Conservative Party', p. 422.
[58] D. R. Thorpe, *Eden: The Life and Times of Anthony Eden, First Earl of Avon, 1897–1977* (Pimlico, 2004), p. 391.
[59] Butler, *The Art of the Possible*, p. 144.
[60] Ramsden, *The Making of Conservative Party Policy*, p. 141.
[61] Butler, *The Art of the Possible*, p. 144.
[62] Butler to David Eccles MP (copy), 27 August 1948, Conservative Research Department papers, CRD 2/23/7.
[63] David Gammans MP to Churchill (copy), 29 January 1948, ibid.
[64] John Ramsden, '"A Party for Owners or a Party for Earners?" How far did the British Conservative Party really change after 1945?', *Transactions of the Royal Historical Society*, Vol. 37 (1987), p. 57.
[65] Conservative Research Department Papers, CRD 2/53/1.

Brendon Sewill
POLICY-MAKING FOR HEATH

BRENDON SEWILL joined the Conservative Research Department in 1952, and was its Director from 1964 until 1970. He moved to the Treasury as Special Assistant to the Chancellor of the Exchequer from September 1970 until March 1974. Thereafter he was Adviser on Public Affairs to the Committee of London and Scottish Bankers (now the British Bankers Association) from 1975 to 1990.

The period 1965–70 saw intense work on policy-making, more than in any previous period of Opposition. This was partly because it was Ted Heath's prime interest, and partly because of the need to dispel the allegation that the Party had run out of steam after thirteen years in government. Yet despite, as Douglas Hurd put it, being 'equipped with policies more elaborate and better researched than any Opposition had ever attempted',[1] it all ended in disaster with the collapse of the Heath Government in less than four years. This account concludes with an attempt to analyse the reasons for the failure of the policies on which we had worked so hard.

The arrival of Ted Heath in charge of policy after the 1964 election, as Chairman of the Party's Advisory Committee on Policy, signalled an abrupt change for the Conservative Research Department. For those of us who had served below decks in 24 and 34 Old Queen Street in the 1950s and early 1960s, the Chairman of the Department, Rab Butler, was an Olympian figure; all we saw of him was a brief descent before Christmas to give us a limp handshake and thank us for our good work. With Heath, frequent meetings were held in the Chairman's room on the third floor of Number 24 or in his Albany flat. My enduring memory of those meetings is of Ted, shoulders shaking with mirth at some arcane joke, making a point of dunking his biscuits in his tea to remind us of his humble origins.

Some politicians are primarily interested in power and see policies as the building bricks on which they climb to the top; others are intensely interested in policy and see politics as a distasteful necessity. Ted Heath belonged to the latter group, along with his colleagues Keith Joseph and Edward Boyle. That he so enjoyed teasing out the detail of each policy attracted great loyalty from those who worked closely with him. But his distaste for politics, with no time for small talk and dislike of having to put complex issues in simple everyday language (I spent hours with him agonising before each television appearance), eventually proved his undoing.

As John Campbell wrote in his excellent biography of Heath: 'His determination that the next Conservative Government should come into office more thoroughly prepared than any in history was to be the central purpose of his leadership over [the years 1965–70]'.[2] Another reason why Ted took such an interest in the details of policy was that, as the first working-class (albeit via Balliol) Leader, he felt he needed to achieve a dominance over his more patrician Shadow Cabinet colleagues; and this he could only do by knowing more about their subjects than they did themselves.

The majority of the members of his Shadow Cabinet were former cabinet ministers, and looked to the Research Department as their shadow civil service. There were no publicly funded research assistants for MPs: all the responsibility for co-ordinating the policy work fell on the Research Department.

At that time the Research Department was proudly separate from Central Office, liked to think of itself as quasi-academic, and was housed in a couple of elegant buildings looking out over St James's Park. We had a staff of around 60 to 70, reaching a peak of 75 in 1970. Half were desk officers, and half support staff – secretaries, librarians, messengers – and telephonists. Those were the days when we had our own plug-in telephone exchange on the top floor of Number 24: one lifted the phone and asked Miss King for the person one wanted.

The way the Department was organised was that each desk officer dealt with one subject, usually coinciding with a government department, and thus worked directly to one member of the Shadow Cabinet. Each had three roles: first, to think about future policy and to act as secretary to the relevant policy group; second, to act as research assistant to the Shadow Minister, to attend the relevant back-bench Parliamentary Committee, and to provide briefs for the Parliamentary Party; and third, to write the relevant sections of Party publications, e.g. *Notes on Current Politics* and *The Campaign Guide*.

There were regular grumbles that the pressures of urgent day-to-day work left insufficient time for research, and some suggestions that the Department should be split into two sections, with one dealing only with research. That I firmly rejected. The system of one officer responsible for all aspects of a subject ensured specialisation and consistency: no time needed to be wasted on liaison. Moreover, dealing with the current battles in Parliament, and even the effort of trying to explain ideas in simple terms to the Party faithful, stimulated ideas for policy initiatives.

The staff consisted of a mixture of old warhorses and bright aspiring politicians fresh from university – mainly Oxbridge and often via the Union. The politically experienced and shrewd warhorses – David Dear, Geoffrey Block, Charles Bellairs, Oliver Stebbings, Tony Greenland – were crucial to maintaining some order and political sense in what was otherwise a potentially chaotic operation. Michael Fraser[*], my predecessor as Director of the Research Department, who had been promoted to Deputy Chairman of the Party, was an excellent mother-in-law: a source of wise advice while never interfering, and a good friend. The warhorses brought long experience too: at the party held in 1969 to mark the fortieth anniversary of the Department, Oliver Stebbings recalled how efficiently the 1931 *Campaign Guide* had been written.

We undertook virtually no original university-style research: our role was to invent solutions to current problems and to put academic ideas into political clothes. Considerable effort went into making the

---

[*]Sir Michael Fraser, later Lord Fraser of Kilmorack.

clothes hang together as part of traditional Tory philosophy. It was our belief that the electorate needed to see a coherent purpose, not just a random collection of good ideas. Conservative principles, and in those days we quoted a good deal of Burke and Disraeli, are sufficiently broad to cover almost any policy. This, however, was a technique which Heath disliked, and which he ignored once he became Prime Minister (the 1972 Industry Act was the classic case) to the consternation of the Party. So far as he was concerned if a policy was sound, that was sufficient.

*

The policy exercise of 1965–70 was co-ordinated by the academic and absent-minded James Douglas, while Michael Spicer* trawled the universities for ideas and for recruits for the policy groups. One has to admit that the aim was not entirely to acquire knowledge: in part it was to make the Party look intellectually respectable.

Because in 1965 the Labour Government had a tiny majority, an election was expected at any moment, and everything started in a great rush. Thirty-six policy groups were set up and most of them had produced reports by the summer. Membership of the policy groups was kept secret, because some businessmen and academics were not prepared to admit in public to assisting the Opposition. The reports were also kept strictly secret. They were shown to the Shadow Minister, if he was not the chairman of the group, and to Heath. After that they went to the Advisory Committee of Policy (consisting of the Party bigwigs with myself as Secretary), and then to the Shadow Cabinet. Most never saw the light of day, but were recast in the form of speeches by Heath.

By July 1965 most of the policy group reports were in my filing cabinet but had not been shown to the Deputy Leader, Reggie Maudling. With the leadership election imminent, he rang me up and asked if he could have a look at them. At first I said, 'yes of course' but when I asked Heath he replied: 'Don't give them to that bloody man, he'll only take credit for them.' So, having consulted Alec Home (who in fact resigned a few days later), I had to write to

---

*Now Sir Michael Spicer, Chairman of the 1922 Committee.

Maudling to postpone my offer[3] – and go into hiding in case he arrived in my office!

At that time there were no great differences of policy or philosophy between Heath and Maudling – certainly I would have been happy working for either. The difference was one of character. As a BBC *Panorama* programme put it: Heath 'thrustful, pugnacious, aggressive'; Maudling 'backed by those who value brain-power above energy, judgement above drive.'[4] In retrospect, if Maudling had become Leader, the policy work would have been much less frenetic. He believed that detailed policy-making was pointless without civil service assistance.

In the winter of 1965–6 there was a public controversy between Maudling and Enoch Powell, with Powell attacking incomes policies, urging drastic cuts in taxation and welfare, and calling for denationalisation; and with Maudling defending the policies of the previous Conservative Government. As David Butler pointed out in his study of the 1970 election, Heath had comparatively little interest in this debate. He 'looked for the solution to the problems of the economy in a different direction which can conveniently (if inadequately) be termed "technocratic"'.[5]

When the election came in March 1966, Heath was determined to prove that the Conservative Party had new ideas. So I was instructed to extract every recommendation from all the policy groups and, after a Sunday at home with a constant supply of wet towels, came up with a manifesto with 131 policies, each one a separate single sentence bullet point. The electorate was unimpressed.

After the election the policy work continued, but with longer to work out the details. The framework had been set: there was no going back to rethink fundamental principles. As the policy groups completed their work the emphasis changed to specific research projects which were either carried out in house or contracted out; for example, on family poverty, on abuses of the social services, on the concept of a negative income tax, on international treaty obligations in relation to agricultural subsidies, and on the East of Suez policy –

how far Britain should commit itself to keeping permanent military presences in the Gulf and in Malaysia. Peter Goldman* was commissioned to do a report into the government of Scotland but his conclusion – that any move towards devolution would lead inexorably towards separation – was not accepted. Instead, in June 1967, a Scottish Policy Group was set up, and was followed by a Constitutional Committee under Alec Home. It reported in early 1970, recommending an elected Assembly to debate the Second Reading and Committee stages of Scottish Bills.

I was fortunate to be awarded a Smith-Mundt fellowship to spend two months in 1967 studying any subject of my choice in the United States. Advised to see as much as I could, I chose the subject of Federal and State Government, and thus visited around 30 States, coming back with a plethora of exciting but mainly useless ideas.

In 1969 Maudling became Chairman of the Advisory Committee on Policy, and I wrote to James Douglas (who was on a sabbatical year as a visiting professor at an American university): 'Reggie Maudling is taking his new responsibility ... quite seriously and comes in here regularly every Friday. He does not like setting up new policy groups but tends to ask the Research Department to produce papers on various aspects of policy'.[6]

Another technique we used was to organise seminars on various subjects, bringing together MPs, academics and businessmen. Several hundred attended each event but tended to get bored if they had no chance to speak. Subjects covered during 1968–9 included economic policy, science and technology, the arts, higher education, and housing, planning and architecture.

Not all the conclusions of the policy groups were accepted.

The tax group came up with the idea of a wealth tax. I recall an intense debate at Swinton College in Yorkshire, where Heath and selected members of the policy groups had gone for a brain-storming

---

*Peter Goldman, a former member of the Research Department, was widely tipped as a future Cabinet Minister until he suffered a spectacular defeat at the 1962 Orpington by-election.

session. Harold Macmillan used to stay there with the Earl of Swinton to shoot grouse: Heath went, as it happened in deep snow, to debate a wealth tax. The idea was shot down, to the huge relief of the Party fund-raisers.

The denationalisation group, with Nick Ridley as chairman and with Tony Newton* as dissenting secretary, came up with a programme of old-fashioned denationalisation which Heath rejected as too doctrinaire. But when it was transmuted into a policy of selling shares to the public, later to become known as privatisation, it began to look more promising. In 1969 Maudling asked Ridley to 'make a study of the possibilities of selling off shares in the nationalised industries.'[7] I followed this up with a meeting with Ridley at his home, where he cooked me an excellent lunch. My comment at the time was that the policy 'seems to me very important and ties up with our other theme of encouraging savings and ownership.' No one at that time predicted that privatisation would have the added bonus of ending many national wage negotiations, thus making inflation much easier to control. Privatisation, however, did not appeal to Heath partly because to him it seemed to have more to do with politics than with improving efficiency, and partly because our programme for the first Parliament was so full that there was no room for any additional controversial legislation.

Throughout the 1960s the Tories were looking for a distinctive stance on the social services, and were toying with the idea of replacing the Beveridge concept of universal provision by a policy of concentrating benefits on those in need. But should this apply only to cash benefits or to all types of social services, such as free education and free health? And how could we get away from the need for multiple means tests? Due to the political sensitivity of these issues a rather secret Social Priorities Working Party[8] was set up in 1967 with myself as chairman; the members included Maurice Macmillan and Paul Dean[†], with Norman Lamont[‡] as secretary. Keith Joseph and Margaret Thatcher were semi-detached members,

---

* Now Lord Newton of Braintree.
† Later Lord Dean of Harptree.
‡ Now Lord Lamont of Lerwick.

attending some of our meetings, commenting on our report but not actually signing it, thus perhaps demonstrating an early desire for more radical measures.

We found good reasons for not converting the health service to an insurance scheme; rejected educational vouchers; turned down charges for hospital treatment; preferred private hospitals to private beds in NHS hospitals; supported charges for nursery schools, and charges for school meals and milk (thus landing Margaret Thatcher, when she became Education Secretary, with being labelled 'milk-snatcher Thatcher'). We wanted to see housing subsidies attached to the family instead of to the (council) house; favoured some modest tax relief for private education and health preferably through a general tax relief for savings; and welcomed the concept of a link between the social services and the income tax system.

The concept of a negative income tax, in which people filled in an annual tax return, paid tax if their income was above tax level, but received benefits only if their income was below benefit level, seemed an elegant solution to the Tory desire to reduce taxation and concentrate benefits only on those in need. While in the United States, I explored the work done there; Barney Hayhoe* developed the idea of paying family allowances only to those below tax level and published his conclusions in a pamphlet *Must the children suffer?* in 1969; and we inserted a positive reference into the 1970 manifesto, together with the comment that: 'The Government has exaggerated the administrative problems involved.'

Renamed a tax credit scheme, the idea was developed in a Green Paper published by Tony Barber in 1973, but it still bristled with administrative problems. With the defeat of the Heath Government it went into cold store, was rejected by Margaret Thatcher as vaguely socialist ('to each according to his means'), but re-emerged as the Child Tax Credit, the Working Tax Credit and the Pension Tax Credit schemes introduced by Gordon Brown in 2003. Some policies have a long gestation period and a mixed-up pedigree.

---

* Now Lord Hayhoe.

Then, as now, Europe was a difficult issue. There was no appetite for exploring the pros and cons rationally and in depth: they depended too much on gut feelings of revulsion at the carnage of two World Wars and, on the other side, dreams that the Commonwealth could recreate the glories of the British Empire.

Heath never had any doubt that we must join. The Foreign Affairs Policy Group, chaired by Alec Home, confirmed support for joining. Thus our official policy remained unchanged, unlike that of the Labour Party which swung back and forth: in opposition against, in government for.

Public opinion was equally fickle. In 1966 I reported that: 'Our polls showed that ... three times as many people were *for* joining the Common Market as were *against*.'[9] By 1970 the polls showed most people opposed to entry. Yet in the 1975 referendum the vote was two to one in favour. Within the Party opinion was divided, with some of the loudest voices being opposed. When Geoffrey Tucker, head of publicity at Central Office, asked my advice in August 1969 about a proposed leaflet on the Common Market, I replied 'You will appreciate that this is an extremely difficult subject for the Conservative Party to publish anything official on at this stage. We don't want to do anything which might precipitate a revolt at the Party Conference. On the other hand there is a steady stream of requests for information'.[10] My advice was to publish the leaflet but not draw it to the attention of the press.

*

Preparing for government is not like academic research which can be done in comparative peace: it is more like an army having to regroup under fire. There were constant enquiries from the media to be fended off; debates in Parliament where the Party line had to be decided; twice weekly (in those days) Prime Minister's Questions; and 300 Members of Parliament to be kept in line. As now, the pressure was great for an Opposition to oppose everything unpopular the Government did. That led Iain Macleod, for example, to oppose incomes policies when at that time we had no alternative way of stopping inflation.

I attended all meetings of the Shadow Cabinet and briefed the Department on my return. Like good civil servants, Research Department officers expressed their views strongly in advance but then accepted the Shadow Cabinet decisions. Only one officer resigned on a policy issue: as a former colonial civil servant, he wanted the Conservatives to support sending in British troops to depose Ian Smith after he had declared unilateral independence for Rhodesia, the opposite view to that taken by most Conservative rebels –who wished to support Smith.

Nor could all MPs be kept in line. The prime example in those years was Enoch Powell. As a former member of the Department, Enoch was a good friend, but a thorn in Ted Heath's side on many issues other than immigration. He was a severe critic of any argument, on incomes policy, or the nuclear deterrent, or East of Suez, which did not live up to his precise, some would say pedantic, standard of logic. So we were sad when he put himself beyond the pale. The trouble with Enoch was that he started from a premise and pursued it logically to a conclusion. Thus a high level of immigration led inexorably to 'rivers of blood'. When he had been Minister of Health he had (logically) clamped down excessively hard on nurses' pay because an increase would have exceeded his budget; but when he was in free market mode he attacked incomes policies (logically) as 'dangerous nonsense' for attempting to limit public sector pay. In the real world politics is about making a compromise between the many premises from which to start a deduction.

Heath's bachelor status and his addiction to policy meant that, unless he was sailing, my weekends were never safe from interruption. But in terms of staff, I had it easy. If I needed an extra researcher, I only had to ask and the Party Treasurers were told to stump up.

The Treasurers did not love the Research Department. We tried to help by producing an illustrated booklet, *Behind the door of Number*

*Door of 24 Old Queen Street, London SW1,
the Department's home until 1979.*

Neville Chamberlain
Chairman of the Conservative Research Department 1930-40

(Portrait painted in 1929, the year of CRD's foundation, by Sir William Orpen: formerly in the possession of Mrs Frank Chamberlain, now part of the Parliamentary Art Collection)

THE ARCHITECTS OF POST-WAR TORY POLICY

Rab Butler
Chairman of the Conservative Research Department 1945-64
(reproduced from a CRD photograph)

David Clarke
Director of the Conservative Research Department 1945-51
(Conservative Party Archive)

POLICY MAKERS OF THE LATE 1960s

*Brendon Sewill (Director, 1964-70),
Enoch Powell (former CRD officer; Conservative
Spokesman on Defence, 1965-68), and
Tim Boswell (CRD officer, 1966-73;
now MP for Daventry)*

*Michael Fraser
(Director, 1951-64;
Chairman, 1970-74)*

*Discussing economic issues: (left to right) Peter Bocock (later a senior economist with the
World Bank), John Cope (later MP and Minister; now Lord Cope of Berkeley),
Iain Macleod (former CRD officer; Shadow Chancellor of the Exchequer, 1965-70)
and the back of Brendon Sewill, in 24 Old Queen Street*
(Pictures from *Behind the Door of 24 Old Queen Street*; see p. 65)

CELEBRATING FORTY YEARS OF CRD

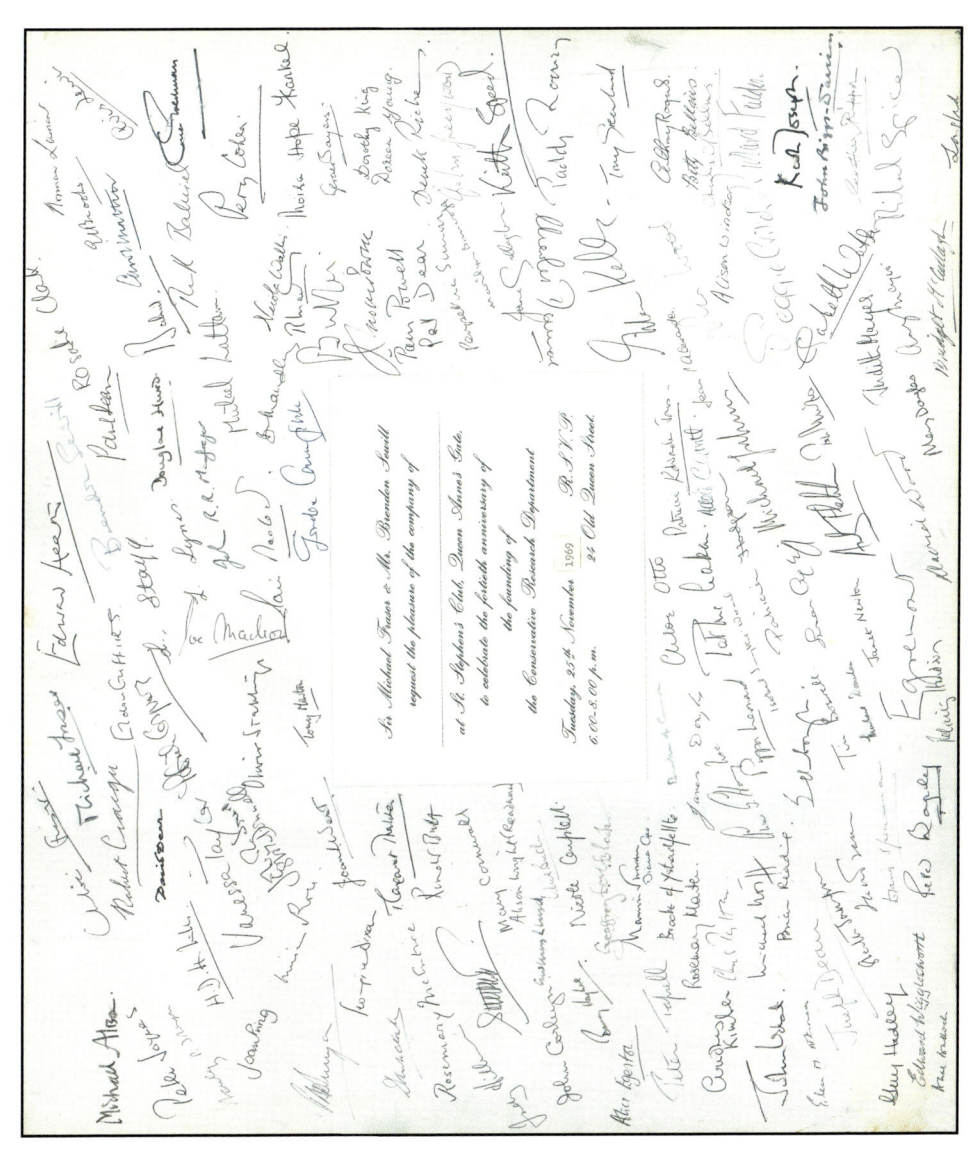

Edward Heath was the principal guest at a fortieth anniversary party which was also attended by his successor as Conservative leader, Margaret Thatcher, distinguished CRD graduates including Henry Brooke, Iain Macleod and Enoch Powell, the great post-war Chairman, Rab Butler, and other members of the Department, past and present, some of whom, like Douglas Hurd and Norman Lamont, would be government ministers in the future.
(Conservative Party Archive)

THE PARTY LEADER AND HER CRD DIRECTOR BEFORE THE 1979 ELECTION

(Conservative Party Archive)

CONSERVATIVE RESEARCH DEPARTMENT
The Carlton Club ~ 22 June 2006

Back row, left to right
Richard Parr (International Development), James North (formerly Transport), Denzil Davidson (Europe), Douglas McNeill (Head of Economic Section), Bill Morgan (Health), Chris Cook (Treasury), Glyn Gaskarth (Home Affairs), Richard Hardyment (Political Section), Garvan Walshe (Foreign Affairs), Adam Buckley (Intern Co-ordinator)

Fourth row, left to right
Graham Hook (Home Affairs), Tara Singh (DEFRA), Vita Maynard (Transport), Stephen Parkinson (Political Section)

Third Row, left to right
Lucy Lee (Public Services Policy Group and CPF), Cllr Nigel Fletcher (Education), Nick Park (Trade and Industry), Sam Talbot Rice (DCMS)

Second row, left to right
Chris Newton (Defence), Sian Jones (Work and Pensions)

Front row, left to right
Jonathan Caine (Assistant Director and Northern Ireland/Constitution), Alistair Cooke OBE (Editor and former Deputy Director), Cllr Sheridan Westlake (Assistant Director and Local Government), Oliver Dowden (Head of Political Section), John Glen (Director).

*Conservative Central Office, 32 Smith Square, London SW1,
the Department's home from 1979 to 2004.*
(It is now housed in the Conservative Campaign Headquarters at 30 Millbank, SW1.)

24, describing the work of the Department, which we hoped would enable them to raise more funds from businessmen. It contained rather a good picture of Enoch Powell, Tim Boswell[*] and me (reproduced amongst the illustrations between pages 64 and 65). Central Office refused to use it. A few months later, when Enoch had become a non-person, it had to be pulped.

In those pre-computer and pre-photocopier days, the secretaries were vital to our operation. They were all highly respectable, highly competent and highly intelligent young ladies. I should know, I married one. So did Enoch Powell and several other colleagues. The secretaries needed to be intelligent to understand their subject so as to be able to make sense of their shorthand notes, and competent because they had to type at 60 words a minute with six carbon copies and no mistakes. Although it may nowadays sound rather chauvinistic, dictating to a pretty and attentive female was a remarkably good stimulus to a fine turn of phrase. And a raised eyebrow prevented many a howler.

They were hand-picked by the indomitable personnel officer, Avis Lewis (and had to show their pluck by facing her equally indomitable Great Dane). She had old-fashioned views: one day she arrived in my office in a state of shock to say that some girls had come in wearing skirts *above the knee*, and that she was proposing to send them home immediately. Thus our preparations for government were nearly halted by the advent of the swinging sixties.

Douglas Hurd[†], Brian Reading and Michael Wolff all joined the Department in the autumn of 1966, recruited by Heath to form his own *cabinet*. Hurd came as a fully fledged high-flying Foreign Office diplomat, always ultra-intelligent, ultra-urbane. Brian Reading came as an academic economist disillusioned after a stint in George Brown's Department of Economic Affairs, while Michael Wolff was a journalist who became Ted Heath's chief speech-writer and closest confidant. I made myself unpopular with Heath when I refused his request that the three of them should sit in a separate room, perhaps in a separate building, and not be bothered by day-to-day Research

---
[*] Now MP for Daventry.
[†] Now Lord Hurd of Westwell.

Department business. I still have my pencil note of his words: 'Well you must organise it as you think best, but try to get this done. It must be done'. My reason for refusing was that the Department was there to serve the whole Party, and the whole Shadow Cabinet, and also that there would be mutual benefit in cross-fertilisation of ideas. I got my way, and indeed Douglas Hurd acted as head of our foreign affairs section for a time, and Brian Reading serviced the Economic Policy Group. But from then on, and also perhaps on account of my agnosticism on Europe, Heath never quite counted me as 'one of us'.

The Research Department always had a close relationship with Heath's private office. John MacGregor*, who was in charge of the private office from 1965 to 1969, came via the Research Department. Douglas Hurd took over the private office in September 1969 and, of course, continued as Heath's Political Secretary in Number 10 until the 1974 debacle.

Miles Hudson, who followed Hurd as head of our foreign affairs section, was a former army officer who had been a liaison officer with the Russian army, and was thus used to dangerous missions. While he was with us, he took his Shadow Minister Lord Carrington into the rebel Biafra during the Nigerian civil war, landing at night without lights to dodge the anti-aircraft fire. Not all our preparations for government were quite so daring.

Since we were all paid out of Party funds, the salaries on offer were not sufficient to attract many experienced people in mid-career, so I relied mainly on young men (and the occasional young woman) straight from university. Thus at the end of 1965 I recruited a young man who had recently come down from Oxford, and reported to Michael Fraser that: 'I would really prefer someone a little older and more experienced but I think Patten† could develop quite well'.[11]

New raw recruits got allocated to any post that happened to be vacant. Thus I wrote to Sir John Gilmour, Chairman of the Party in Scotland: 'I have now got a new young man who will be taking over responsibility for Scottish Affairs in this office. His name is Chris

---

* Now Lord MacGregor of Pulham Market.
† Now Lord Patten of Barnes.

Patten. I am afraid he has not got Scottish connections but he has come down from Oxford with a very good history degree and he has spent some time working in John Lindsay's team in the New York election. He is quick, bright and writes well.' [12]

And on the same day I wrote to Sir Keith Joseph: 'I have now got a young man to take over responsibility in this office for pensions and [in due course] for health as well. His name is Norman Lamont. He has got a degree in economics from Cambridge, [and] was President of the Cambridge Union ... He is keen to do research and I hope you will find him useful'.

We were never short of talent. Stanley Johnson arrived in 1969 with an eclectic combination of qualifications: a member of his college rugby team, the Newdigate prize for poetry, a degree in agricultural economics, experience working for the World Bank – and the same irreverent sense of humour as his son Boris. He pioneered the subject of the environment, playing an important part in the decision in 1970 to set up the new Department of the Environment.

Hurd, Lamont, MacGregor, Newton and Patten all went on to become long-serving members of Margaret Thatcher's Cabinet, and were also members of John Major's Cabinet. John Cope* who joined us as a young accountant in March 1965 (finding himself immediately embroiled in the controversial Finance Bill on which Ted Heath was making the running) went on to become Paymaster General and later Opposition Chief Whip in the Lords. Many others made it into the lower reaches of government.

Not all went into Parliament. Stanley Johnson became head of the European Commission Environment Division and subsequently an MEP. When Patricia Hodgson† arrived fresh from Newnham in September 1968 I allocated her the job of desk officer for the Post Office and broadcasting, which led on to a distinguished career in the BBC: she is now Principal of her old college. John McDonnell had the task of coping with the fall-out from Enoch Powell's 'rivers of blood' speech, and survived to be a leading QC. Stephen

---

* Now Lord Cope of Berkeley.
† Now Dame Patricia Hodgson.

Sherbourne* joined in January 1970 with (according to my notes) 'no political experience' but went on to rectify that by becoming head of Margaret Thatcher's political office. Patrick Cosgrave was almost the only one who did not develop a sense of loyalty to Heath: he became political editor of *The Spectator* and a fierce critic of the Heath Government. On reflection it was a mistake to allocate him to do the briefing for Prime Minister's Question Time: a loquacious Irishman did not hit it off with a prickly Heath apprehensive of being made fun of yet again by Harold Wilson.

In a passage I wrote for the Party Chairman's speech at the 1969 conference, I was able to claim that there had been over 50 major policy groups, and over 2,000 papers had been circulated. 'It is part of the preparation for government to ensure that the policies we propose are both foolproof, and ready to be put into effect when we return to power. It is most important that the next Conservative Government should not waste its first year'.[13]

Fifty policy groups, but were the policies consistent, were they ready to be put into action, which of them should be legislated in the first year, could they all be done in one Parliament? It was difficult to get these big issues discussed at the weekly meetings of the Shadow Cabinet where the debate tended to concentrate on the immediate issues before Parliament. James Douglas and I therefore hit on the wheeze of locking the Shadow Cabinet up for a weekend until they reached conclusions.

The Selsdon Park Hotel near Croydon was chosen for the lock-up. The agenda included health, pensions, family allowances, economic policy, controlling prices, should Britain attempt to maintain a military force east of Suez, a review of all commitments made since 1964, an assessment of the political situation, the draft manifesto, the legislative programme, and which policies should be published.

The conclusion was to go for the lot. Some critics have subsequently argued that the Heath Government tried to do too much at once. Certainly that was the lesson which Margaret Thatcher took on board. She implemented much the same policies, but more gradually.[14]

---

* Now Sir Stephen Sherbourne.

The apogee of all our research was the legislative programme for the first year of the new Parliament. Typed on large sheets of paper (spread-sheets were unknown in those days) it showed, week by week: first, the dates of known events such as the day fixed for changing to a decimal currency; second, Parliamentary business – with proposed dates for introducing a score of Bills; third, suggested dates for Government announcements; and fourth, the timetable for drafting legislation.

I delivered the final version of this document to 10 Downing Street on the evening after polling day. Heath had just arrived after visiting the Queen. I knocked on the door (in those days there were no security barriers, anyone could walk down Downing Street), and handed the envelope in. Although I had worked so closely with Heath for nearly six years, I did not go in. Instinctively I realised that he would have already moved into governmental mode, would be wishing to talk to the head of the civil service, putting the distasteful necessity of politics behind him.

*

So why is the preparation for the Heath Government hardly ever written up as the heyday of the Research Department?

One reason is that history is written by the victors. In the 1950s Butler, Maudling, Macleod and Powell had every reason to talk up the brilliance of the post-war Department. By contrast Margaret Thatcher's political imperative was to emphasise her clean break with the past. She had no love for the Research Department, seeing it as a nest of Keynesian Heathite wets. Those who moved from the Research Department into Parliament had to undergo a long process of decontamination. In the 1983 *Campaign Guide* Heath's name only appeared once in the index.

The more important reason why little credit is given to the 1965–70 period is, of course, that it all went wrong. The dramatic failure of the Heath Government meant that no one could take pride in having produced its policies. Why did a Government so well prepared not succeed in staying in power?

First, as every dear boy knows, events. No one knew that Iain Macleod would die or Maudling resign. Although I believe that had Macleod remained as Chancellor his policies would have been the same as those pursued by Tony Barber, he had the ability to inspire the public which both Heath and Barber lacked. No one predicted that Rolls Royce would go bust. No one envisaged the Middle East war and the oil crisis which enabled the coal miners to hold the country to ransom. With hindsight, we should have had a policy group on crisis management. A good deal of work had been done on the machinery of government by Mark Schreiber[*] and David Howell[†], but it was all about improving civil service efficiency not how to handle what became an almost continuous crisis from 1972 to 1974.

The plans for trade union reform were too legalistic. In 1965 the Shadow Cabinet had a series of private dinners at the St Stephen's Club in order to have a relaxed discussion of policy. On one such occasion I recall a rumbustious dissertation by Quintin Hogg on the need for a comprehensive Industrial Relations Act to do for trade unions what the Companies Act of 1862 did for companies. That set the pattern. The Trade Union Policy Group was stuffed with lawyers, but had few economists. The result was the Industrial Relations Act, a magnificent legal edifice with no policy to deal with strikes by miners, electricity workers, railwaymen and other groups who in those days had the power to bring the country to a standstill. There was some hope that, while the unions would oppose the Bill, once it was passed by Parliament they would acquiesce. No such luck. The moral was learnt by Margaret Thatcher: don't base your policies on optimism; build up a stock of coal.

The one policy that did work was getting Britain into Europe. There is a debate among the intelligentsia whether major political changes come about as a result of the personal action of politicians or whether they are part of an inexorable historical process. Certainly it was my impression that our entry into the European Common Market on 1 January 1973 would not have happened if it had not

---

[*] Now Lord Marlesford.
[†] Now Lord Howell of Guildford.

been for Ted Heath's personal determination. Opinion in both the Research Department and the Shadow Cabinet was that the arguments for and against were evenly balanced.

A Party seeking election ideally needs what the Victorians called 'a cry', that is a cause that they feel passionate about, and pledge to put right. Merely to present a series of disconnected initiatives creates no inspiration. Yet we could never claim entry into the Common Market as our main 'cry', partly because it was controversial, and partly because Harold Wilson had switched from opposing it to a half-hearted attempt at entry, but more because it was not within the power of the British Government to deliver. It all depended on whether the French would repeat their veto for a third time. As with climate change today, it was difficult to go into an election with your main policy aim not within your sole control.

*

Economic policy was where the Heath Government came unstuck. The years from 1970 to 1974 saw almost continuous strikes, rising inflation, a succession of incomes policies, each of which failed to stem the rising tide of wage demands, leading eventually to the three-day week – and an election on the theme of who was to govern Britain. To which question, as Andrew Marr put it recently, the electorate gave the answer: 'not you, chum.' (Actually that is a simplification: in February 1974 Heath won a majority of votes, but not of seats.)

The failure of economic policy was predictable, and indeed predicted.

In my report on the 1966 election I commented that: 'It was clear during the campaign and in drafting the Manifesto that the major gap in our policies was that of economic policy.' The polls showed that 'the cost of living was the most important issue when people are deciding how to vote. Yet our own policy was not far enough developed for us to be able to put forward proposals to stop the rise in prices.'[15]

In those days Keynes ruled. The prevailing orthodoxy among academic economists, the Treasury, press and politicians was that the economy should be run at a high level of demand so that everyone who wanted a job could find one. If trade unions used their muscle on an industry-wide basis to push up wage rates and thus prices, this should be dealt with by some form of incomes policy. Monetarism as a political philosophy had not been invented. Milton Friedman was virtually unknown.

But there were a number of British economists who were moving in that direction. As far back as November 1964, when I was head of the economic section of the Research Department, I prepared a paper for the Shadow Cabinet on the balance of payments, the main issue in the recent election, in which I mentioned that 'one [academic] school of thought would see the solution as being to run the economy permanently on a lower level of demand, with unemployment varying between 2 per cent in summer and 3 per cent in winter ... [This would make] an incomes policy easier to implement – indeed almost unnecessary.'[16]

We returned to the issue some years later. With help from Tony Newton and Brian Reading, I prepared a paper entitled 'The Cost of Living' and in January 1968 sent it to Heath[17], recognising that it was 'advocating major changes in our Conservative economic policy', and requesting that it should be considered by the Economic Policy Group and by the Shadow Cabinet. In it we reviewed current academic thinking on price stability and recommended:

- running the economy at an unemployment rate of 2 to 2.5 per cent;
- raising interest rates to create a short sharp deflation to reach this level;
- trade union reform;
- a firm government line on wage claims in the public sector; and
- being prepared to face and win a major strike.

Apart from the fact that there was no mention of the word 'monetarism' and no mention of Milton Friedman, the policy was almost identical to that pursued by Thatcher and Howe in 1979–83.

Heath ignored it. The Economic Policy Group, with Ted Heath as chairman and Arthur Cockfield (a former Inland Revenue Commissioner) as one of the leading members, concentrated largely on tax and avoided the issue of economic management.

Eighteen months later we regurgitated the paper and sent it to Heath and Maudling.[18] Neither followed it up. A few extracts give the flavour: 'Polls show the cost of living is the most important political issue. Recent ... academic work [indicates that] ... no Government stands a chance of preventing prices rising if unemployment is below 2 per cent ... remarkable uniformity of [academic] view that if unemployment ... about 2 ½ per cent, ... if control of money supply ... and if Government can influence "cost push" factors, prices can be expected to remain steady.' The paper then went on to examine how a future Government could influence the cost-push effect of trade union national bargaining.

At the Selsdon conference a summary of the paper was circulated, but was passed over quickly. At the time I put this down to Heath's reluctance to open up a division between Maudling (who was in favour of a formal incomes policy) and Macleod (who was not). Neither Keith Joseph nor Margaret Thatcher showed any interest in it – their conversion to monetarism came after the 1974 debacle.

I was sufficiently worried that, in March 1970, six weeks after Selsdon and not knowing that we were only weeks away from an election, I sent what I called 'a provocative note' to Heath. Extracts again give the feel: 'I am extremely worried that, despite all the work done on other aspects of economic policy, we have no policy for restraining the level of prices, and apparently no desire to get one ... It is probably true that we can get through the next election by abusing the Labour Government; but if the next Conservative Government is going to preside over an even more rapid inflation it will soon find itself extremely unpopular ... [Some Conservative policies will put up prices] ... If we have no other solution we will inevitably in due course be forced back to the old-fashioned stop-go with heavy increases in taxation. Bang go all our hopes of creating an atmosphere of expansion ... Muddle and ineffectiveness over prices and incomes policy has proved the undoing of the past two

Administrations, and at the present rate I cannot see how the next Conservative Administration is going to create a reputation for competence in this field.'[19]

Admiral Heath put his telescope to his blind eye, and did not reply.

Thus, as I wrote in my report after the 1970 election: 'The result was that the Research Department had, at the very last moment, to invent a policy for dealing with inflation; and this was spatchcocked into the manifesto after the seventh draft when it was in its final proof stage'. I still have a copy of the proofs which I took to the printers with the new page attached with a rusty paper clip. The new policy included the sentence: 'We utterly reject the philosophy of compulsory wage control' – words which came back to haunt us when in 1972 it proved impossible to stop inflation without statutory wage controls. Brian Reading was so concerned about the lack of a credible policy that in the last week of the 1970 election he wrote a speech for Heath containing proposals to reduce the rise in prices 'at a stroke'. Heath never delivered the speech but got saddled with the quote.

Why was the issue of inflation never resolved? Partly it was personalities: Ted Heath was not an economist, had never been a Treasury Minister and disliked the Treasury; his only ministerial experience in the economic field had been as Secretary of State for Industry, Trade and Regional Development. The Deputy Leader, Reggie Maudling, had been a competent Chancellor of the Exchequer, but having not been elected Leader nor given the job of Shadow Chancellor, tended to take a back seat. Macleod, as his biographer put it, 'was never entirely at home with the problems of the economy'.[20] Heath's main interest was in improving industrial efficiency. He too easily absorbed the case pressed on him by business leaders that economic growth depended on running the economy constantly at full blast, and that 'stop-go' budgets had weakened business confidence and reduced long-term investment. As Douglas Hurd wrote: 'This doctrine ... was dinned into his ears [by businessmen] as Leader of the Opposition from 1966–70. It appealed to his underlying belief in courage and a readiness to take the long view as the prime qualities in politics'.[21]

It would, however, be unfair lay all the blame on Heath and his colleagues: at that time virtually no one realised that – in conditions of full employment with militant and monopolistic trade unions – Keynesian theory had become kaput. The policy, which the Research Department paper put forward, of deliberately increasing the level of unemployment, was abhorrent to a generation of politicians whose beliefs were formed by mass unemployment of the 1930s. For them deliberately to throw men out of work, men whom they had fought alongside in the war, in order to tame the unions, was unthinkable. It took the Machiavellian genius of Friedman, and his disciples in the Institute of Economic Affairs, to give 'sound money' a theological flavour.

At the time, and for a good many years after, I was frustrated, puzzled and annoyed that we had failed on this crucial issue. During our five years in Opposition every other policy was gone over in great detail, but the central issue, on which the Heath Government was to be crucified, was suppressed.

I have come to see, however, that for Heath it was a choice – a tragic choice between Europe and political survival.

Our Research Department proposals for price stability included postponing two specific policies – a change from subsidies for agriculture to import levies, and the introduction of VAT. We argued that these should be postponed because they would increase the price index and stoke inflation. But Heath knew that both policies were essential if he was to persuade the French that we were sufficiently European-minded.

What I did not fully realise was Heath's vision that if Britain was to take its rightful place as the leader of Europe, it was essential that our businesses should be ready to conquer the new European markets; that at the time of joining our businessmen should be confident; that the British economy should be moving upwards. Our proposals for a short sharp deflation, and for running the economy at a lower level of demand, ran directly contrary to that vision.

The vision became more apparent in the early months of 1972. Tony Barber and all his Treasury advisers, including myself, wanted a neutral budget. But we were overruled by Heath. He insisted on tax cuts so that Britain could enter Europe (in January 1973) on a rising curve of confident business expansion. Perhaps Barber should have resigned but he recognised that it was the prerogative of the Prime Minister to dictate the policy for joining the European Community. Since joining was a policy which Barber fully supported, he accepted that this should take priority.

So was born the 'Barber boom' which led on, through the statutory incomes policy, to the miners' strike, the three-day week, and the demise of the Heath Government. The concept of the rising curve of business expansion had never been discussed by any policy group or by the Shadow Cabinet.

Heath succeeded in his prime aim: he succeeded in what he saw as his historic mission to take Britain into the European Community. But in achieving that he created his own nemesis. Like the ancient mariner, having at last brought his ship into port, he became condemned to trudge the world a tragic and lonely figure.

These days it is too easy to demonise Heath and canonise Margaret Thatcher. But throughout the 1965–70 period he had the full support of his Shadow Cabinet, and the same support from his Cabinet throughout all the fraught days of the 1970–74 Government. They were a loyal team inspired by his constant, if at times rather trying, determination to put nation above Party.

Were we at fault in our preparations for government? Margaret Thatcher's acolytes subsequently liked to blame Heath and Barber for not adopting a strict monetarist stance. Although our paper on 'The Cost of Living' suggested a shift in that direction, throughout the period from 1965 to 1970 I do not recall hearing a single Conservative politician challenge the Keynesian orthodoxy. Not Thatcher, not Keith Joseph, nor anyone else. Enoch Powell and the Institute of Economic Affairs were at that time pursuing *laissez faire* policies of smaller government, lower taxes and private welfare, but not monetarism.[22] We launched our little Cost of Living ship ten years before the tide of history turned.

In the 1930s it had taken the revulsion at mass unemployment and the Jarrow March to bring forth Keynes, and ten further years before his theory was adopted in the 1944 Employment White Paper and implemented through the 1946 nationalisation of the Bank of England. That demoted the old gold standard economics, and gave full employment a higher priority than price stability. It took the defeat of Heath by the miners and the 1979 winter of discontent before the political establishment and the British people were prepared to reverse the priorities and abandon full employment. As today with climate change, it was not possible to convince the public of the need to sacrifice dearly held beliefs or cut back comfortable living standards until after disaster had struck.

Notes

A detailed academic account of the work done by the Research Department in 1965-70 is contained in *The Making of the Conservative Party Policy: The Conservative Research Department since 1929* by John Ramsden (Longman, 1980). John Campbell, in his excellent biography *Edward Heath* (Jonathan Cape, 1993), gives a broader assessment of Ted Heath's character, and of the successes and failures of his preparations for government.

This is more a personal reminiscence. I have not gone back to the Research Department files in the Bodleian but have relied mainly on my personal correspondence files, and a few other papers, which have been stored for the past forty years in my garden shed. Any gaps in my account can be blamed on the mice and squirrels who have found the files a cosy place to nest.

[1] Douglas Hurd, *An End to Promises* (Collins, 1979).
[2] John Campbell, *Edward Heath* (Jonathan Cape, 1993).
[3] Letter book, 20 July 1965.
[4] BBC *Panorama*, 26 July 1965, quoted in Campbell, *Edward Heath*.
[5] David Butler & Michael Pinto-Duschinsky, *The British General Election of 1970* (Macmillan, 1971).
[6] Letter book, 28 April 1969.
[7] Letter book, 10 February 1969.

[8] Annual Report, 14 July 1967.
[9] Research Department report on the 1966 Election, 28 April 1966.
[10] Letter book, 27 August 1969.
[11] Letter book, 16 December 1965.
[12] Letter book, 14 January 1966.
[13] Letter book, 4 September 1969.
[14] Geoffrey Howe has commented that 'the Heath manifesto was not as far from the 1979 manifesto as is sometimes believed' (*Contemporary Record*, Summer 1995).
[15] Research Department report on the 1966 General Election, 28 April 1966.
[16] Letter book, November 1964.
[17] Letter book, 10 January 1968.
[18] Letter book, 27 June 1969.
[19] Letter book, 4 March 1970.
[20] Nigel Fisher, *Iain Macleod* (Deutsch, 1973).
[21] Hurd, *An End to Promises*.
[22] Alan Walters's first Institute of Economic Affairs booklet was on freight transport: he did not write his first IEA booklet on monetarism until 1969.

Chris Patten
THE THATCHER YEARS

CHRIS PATTEN worked in the Research Department for four years before the 1970 election; he was its Director from 1974 until 1979. His subsequent career took him to the Cabinet as Secretary of State for the Environment (1989–90) and Party Chairman (1990–2), to Hong Kong as its last Governor (1992–7) and to the European Commission where he had responsibility for foreign affairs (1999–2004). His most recent book, What Next? Surviving the Twenty-First Century, *was published last year.*

I first met Margaret Thatcher when I was a young member of the Home Affairs Section in the Conservative Research Department in the Opposition years between 1966 and 1970. She seemed to be a more regular visitor to Old Queen Street than any of her Shadow Cabinet colleagues, arriving in the tiny office at the top of Number 34 occupied by the Section's head, Charles Bellairs, and his deputy, Tony Greenland. Margaret was invariably clutching a pile of papers – amendments to Parliamentary Bills, articles torn out of *The Daily Telegraph*, stockbrokers' letters – which would have prompted her latest need to consult two men whom she patently liked even as she sought to tear their usually cautious advice to shreds. Charles was a more natural sympathiser, being an instinctive *Telegraph* Conservative. He had a huge affection for Margaret, even as – his voice soaring and wavering like some exotic calling bird – he tried to rein in her latest bright ideas on national insurance or the old age pension. Tony's enthusiasm was more nuanced. He was a great fan of Edward Boyle, her predecessor as Shadow Education Secretary, and bore some of the scars of battles over the 11-plus and the future of grammar schools. His admiration for 'the lady' was touched by wry amusement at her all-guns-blazing approach to most arguments. He plainly thought that she was a bit of a card.

Looking back, what most strikes me about those early recollections is, first, how much Margaret Thatcher was interested in ideas and what has come to be called policy-wonkery. She was especially knowledgeable about, and interested in, the impact of any and every policy change or proposal on the standard and quality of life of what she sometimes called 'our people' – the strivers who adventitiously were strongly represented among floating voters in marginal constituencies. As I will note later, it was forgetting much of what she knew about these people (which was far more than any other politician I have met ever knew) that calamitously proved her undoing. Second, she did not mind disagreement or argument. Indeed, she often seemed disappointed if her latest idea met quiet acquiescence. But if you argued with her then or subsequently, without much knowledge of what you were talking about, then heaven help you. Even more than sloppy thinking, she disliked well-meaning impossibilism. 'The voters won't stand for that', or 'the papers will savage that idea' were not with her the knock-down arguments that they prove so often to be with other politicians. As happens to many leaders, there is a tendency over the years for courtiers and advisers to run scared of disagreeing with the boss, to earn their status by offering a constant murmur of approval, and to join in the collective denunciation of contrary advice or opinions as manifestations of regicide disloyalty. Margaret was not saved from this, but for most of the time I knew and worked for her she had an astonishingly high threshold for contrariness in others. To personalise the point, had this not been true, I would not have been promoted by her four times.

I was asked to become Director of the Conservative Research Department by Michael Wolff, Director-General of the Conservative Party, after the election defeat in February 1974. We knew that another election must be imminent and that there was neither the time nor the inclination to set up an elaborate policy-making exercise. The main strategic objective was to contain the scale of

Labour's advance in an early second election, and in this task we were extremely successful. The Department, under the chairmanship of Ian Gilmour, pulled together the work that emerged from a necessarily limited number of policy groups, with the proposals on the economy largely those that were set out by the Shadow Chancellor Robert Carr in a speech to the candidates' conference on 11 August. The manifesto was drafted mainly by Ian Gilmour and members of the Department. Coming on the heels of the bitterly divisive February election triggered by the miners' strike, and of the post-election discussions with the Liberals on the possibility of forming a coalition, it was studiously moderate in tone while appealing for support against a 'small number of militant extremists.' It stressed the theme of national unity in dealing with inflation and the threat to the nation's democratic institutions. 'If we do not solve our economic problems our political difficulties will be made worse. And if we do not tackle our political problems our economic problems will be insoluble.' The press reaction to this appeal was positive; and while it did not turn the tide in the Party's favour, it did help to mitigate the scale of the probably inevitable defeat.

Turning to this document entitled *Putting Britain First* today, any reader with a sense of what was to come is struck by the extent to which it reflected the contemporary mood of resigned and weary acceptance of the existing economic order, principally the abusive power of trade unions and particularly of a minority of extremists within them. Did we simply settle for managing a country in decline as best we could, with as much comradely bonhomie as was possible (which appeared to be James Callaghan's approach whatever his occasional intellectual flirtations with monetary policy and education reform)? Was there a real danger of relative decline, that is in our national performance compared to that of our competitors, turning to absolute decline with our economy contracting year on year? Even Peter Jenkins, a commentator whose sympathies lay on the centre-left, came to accept this view. Could the trade unions be bribed to moderate their demands by some sort of deal which would give them a stake in national policy-making? The notion of a social contract was to be discredited in time by the growing sense that the unions were made offers that should never have been on the table in return for undertakings that they regularly breached, indeed that we all knew they would breach. What analysis were we to make of the causes of the inflation which, as the October 1974 manifesto averred, threatened catastrophe? Was it solely a monetary phenomenon or was it better controlled by political bargains? Moreover, if monetary policy was the key, could its use, without the reform of union behaviour and the limitation of union power, avoid a destabilising rise in unemployment?

It was hardly surprising that these questions divided the Conservative Party as well as the nation, and the divisions were made more bitter and personal because they became associated with the removal of a leader, Edward Heath, whose unpopularity was not just the result of the loss of three elections out of four, but of an incontinent embrace of disparate political positions and philosophies. Charitably, we should allow for the extraordinary and bruising change in the international economic order that occurred in 1973 with the OPEC oil embargo and the sharp oil price increase. But it was puzzling for an average Party foot-soldier to see the leadership turn itself inside out on economic policy from a vigorous ideological embrace of markets and a comprehensive and legalistic assault on abusive union power to what seemed like full-scale corporatism. Neither appeared to work (not least in electoral terms) and both were presented as if marching orders having been given the only thing for the Party to do was march, gunfire or not:

> 'He's a jolly old chap', said Harry to Jack,
> As they slogged up to Arras with rifle and pack,
> But he did for them both with his plan of attack.

And sometimes, he was not all that jolly.

*

The election of Margaret Thatcher as leader in February 1975 was not in retrospect particularly surprising. As has been argued to the point of cliché she represented the peasants' revolt against the court, the poor bloody infantry against GHQ: the Party leadership had certainly lost touch. Ascending with me in the wheezing and groaning lift at 24 Old Queen Street, our distinguished and familiar visitor Rab Butler – himself one of the greatest policy impresarios the Party has known – asked me, just before the leadership election, 'We don't have to take this Thatcher business seriously do we?' It was what in Latin would have been called a 'num' question.

In addition to being the representative of the Party's backbenchers, Margaret Thatcher was also sustained by an intellectual position that was closely aligned to that of Sir Keith Joseph but more cautiously expressed. Sir Keith had persuaded Heath in May 1974 to allow him to set up the Centre for Policy Studies (CPS) to study the comparative performance of European economies. Thatcher's and Heath's biographer, John Campbell, argues that Heath saw it as a way of keeping Joseph out of mischief. It was soon seen as the focus for intellectual dissent to the official Party view, especially on inflation and the unions. But what was its position when the Party leadership changed and its Vice-Chairman, Margaret Thatcher, herself rose to the purple, and in particular what should be its relationship then with the Research Department which had become her very own?

The Research Department's position was clear. It was not a free-thinking quasi-academic organisation, roaming the highways and byways of intellectual debate with or without publicity and returning from time to time with a fresh idea clenched between its teeth. It was the back-office of the leader and her (or his) chosen Cabinet colleagues. It also served the wider Parliamentary Party principally though the backbench subject committees, and the Party in the country through its work for the Advisory Committee on Policy. The leader is the principal fount of policy, though a wise leader involves colleagues and perhaps gives them a greater sense of this involvement than in reality exists. The Party Conference discusses policy but it does not make it, and the constant repetition of the Conference insistence on a '300,000 houses' pledge in 1950 (probably an ill-conceived allocation of resources) is simply a reminder of the exception that proves the rule.

Following her victory, Margaret Thatcher replaced Ian Gilmour as Chairman of the Research Department with Angus Maude. Sir

Keith Joseph was given overall responsibility for policy and research which he exercised primarily through his chairmanship of the Advisory Committee on Policy and through periodic meetings with me and my deputy, Adam Ridley. He appeared to use the CPS as a sort of private office, a source of ideas and ideological comfort. He did not seek the same detailed leverage over the policy groups that Edward Heath had apparently exercised before the 1966 and 1970 elections. The Research Department worked for the leader and her team. We had similarly worked for her predecessor and his team. This made us suspect to those who saw past policy-making through the prism of dogmatic certainty, and whose ideological drive was frequently rather recent in its attachment to the Conservative cause and was also occasionally infused with conspiracy theory. This made for an uncomfortable relationship with some of those who worked at the CPS, though not with its ever-courteous Chairman. We had to avoid being dragged into the sometimes exaggerated and acrid debates that raged around Thatcher over economic policy, and in particular over the questions of union reform and monetarism.

The leader's own instincts were far more cautious than were those of some who purported to represent the vigorous purity of her position. There was little doubt where she wanted to head, but first the Conservative Party had to win an election. She never ever forgot that. She established an intellectual position that plainly favoured a market approach to economic management, public spending constraint, tax cuts, a greater reliance on monetary policy and trade union reform. The position which we were to adopt by the time of the 1979 election was very different from that in October 1974, and was easier to adumbrate because of the failure of Wilson and Callaghan in the intervening years, especially during the terrible strike-ridden winter of 1978–9. But I do not remember a single occasion when the leader threw caution to the wind and followed the advice to challenge the electorate with the full, unadulterated majesty of the market and monetarist approach of some of her most enthusiastic acolytes. She moved the centre ground of politics in her direction without frightening voters with the prospect of revolutionary change.

I have never before written about the Research Department's relationship with the Centre for Policy Studies. But since others have done so, and given the passage of more than thirty years, I take this opportunity to record how it looked from Old Queen Street. The existence of the CPS was an important part of the way Margaret Thatcher managed the Party. In addition to contributing to a change in political debate and to feeding some of her own enthusiasms, it also satisfied the more ideologically-minded of her supporters that she had not surrendered the flame first lit by Keith Joseph. But the traditional functions and purpose of the Research Department were not changed, and we carefully avoided being drawn into any public scraps with the CPS. I have always shared Lord Fraser's view that the place for back-room boys is in the back-room. So though irritated from time to time, we were never seriously limited or bothered by the activities of the CPS. It did not see itself as a friend; and we did not see it as a serious rival.

There were appropriate liaison arrangements between the two organisations. Keith Joseph, of course, had overall control of policy-making and my deputy at the Research Department, Adam Ridley, sat on the board of the CPS. Adam and I would meet Keith Joseph most weeks to discuss progress; Nick True, a new recruit from Cambridge, took the minutes of these meetings which are doubtless part of the treasure trove of Research Department papers now kept in the Bodleian Library in Oxford. I do not recall the CPS impinging much on the policy groups that were established, nor on the drafting of policy documents. Nor did it play a significant role in the election campaign or in the constituencies.

Some subjects particularly interested the CPS: one was the way unemployment statistics were presented, another – more significantly – the way in which a new Conservative government should set about reforming the unions. This interest culminated in the drafting of a document entitled 'Stepping Stones' about which much has been written over the years, especially by its authors. On the substance, there was little dispute in the Party leadership. We would need to set about dismantling union privileges and reining in union abuses. But the inflexible strategy proposed in 'Stepping Stones' read as though it lay somewhere between a management consultant's brief and a plan of battle. It showed little political understanding or touch; Lord Thorneycroft, the Party Chairman, was the most formidable of its many critics. Moreover, by the time of the election, the terms of political trade on this issue had dramatically changed. The Government's prices and incomes policy had collapsed. Union abuse had swung the argument in favour of reform decisively in the Conservative Party's direction. We had no need to plan for a military-style assault on Congress House and its outlying fortifications. We could proceed by incremental reform rather than head-on attack.

*

The policy work undertaken in this period was less tightly controlled than it had been from 1964–70. There were more policy groups and more backbenchers were involved in them. The leader and her colleagues were happy to let a hundred flowers bloom. All policy work had to be funnelled eventually through the Research Department, the Advisory Committee on Policy, the Shadow Cabinet and an inner group of Margaret Thatcher's most senior colleagues known as the Steering Committee. A policy sub-committee under Keith Joseph, made up of members of the Shadow Cabinet, vetted all policy proposals before their submission to the whole of the shadow team. The sub-committee met in Old Queen Street, often over lunch.

Margaret Thatcher did not impose herself on all the policy work that was going on. She gave her colleagues considerable elbow-room and was selective about her interests and interventions. She was naturally concerned about the big economic issues that were tackled by Geoffrey Howe's Economic Reconstruction Group. But she left subjects like housing and education to the shadow ministers in charge of these subjects. In foreign and security policy, she set out her strong views on the containment of Soviet communism, asserting correctly but not at the time fashionably that this was a moral as well as a strategic issue. Towards the election, with the looming prospect of government responsibility, she took a growing interest in Rhodesia, and her interest in Northern Ireland was doubtless satisfied in his own shadowy way by Airey Neave, who had managed her election campaign and remained a close confidant. I recall few discussions of Europe. Shortly after her election, she had played a fairly prominent part in the 'Yes' campaign in the referendum on membership of the community, while making clear her own disapproval of referendums as a governing device in our Parliamentary system. This was not an easy baptism as Party leader, since her predecessor was heavily involved in the campaign, but she played her part without embarrassment. Thereafter, the relevance of the arguments on monetary integration of Roy Jenkins (President of the European Commission) and others to the need for greater monetary stability was discussed in late 1978, with some recalling the earlier and humiliating British ejection from the so-called European currency 'snake' in 1973. The manifesto, when it came, promised that a Conservative government would work with, rather than against, Britain's Common Market partners to achieve reforms in the Common Agricultural Policy as well as in the Budget and in Fisheries Policy. *Autres temps, autres mœurs!*

Throughout her years as Leader of the Opposition Margaret Thatcher was determined – rightly in my view – to avoid getting drawn or harried into setting out a detailed blueprint of what a Conservative government would do. She believed that, in Opposition, a Party should win the debate about the broad thrust of policy, a task made easier for Conservatives in the late-1970s by the manifest failure of Labour's own policies and of the consensus on which they had been based. A Party should set out in broad terms what it intended to do, with enough detail on some issues to give credibility to the whole enterprise. But to go further than this ran two risks in her judgement: first, your opponents would simply steal your best ideas; secondly, they would lambast you for those that might be necessary but were at first blush unpopular. This still strikes me as a sound approach. Opposition Parties are always scolded for not having a precise policy for everything. The sensible ones keep as much of their powder dry as possible. Government and Opposition are different. A Government has to react to every event and that becomes its policy. The worst of being in Opposition is not being responsible; an Opposition Party should not be expected to behave as though it were in government, while lacking every advantage and trapping of the real thing. David Cameron is not the first Leader of the Opposition to note that Governments are paid to answer questions, Oppositions to ask them.

Nevertheless, an Opposition Party does need to have a clear narrative which gives an understandable and believable account of what it wants to do and how it differs from the incumbent administration. Margaret Thatcher did this brilliantly, and her personal narrative appeared to exemplify that of her Party. She stood for some simple virtues – hard work, prudence, reward, individual responsibility. These could easily be caricatured by opponents as southern and middle-class. This showed how out of touch they were. On council estates where tenants wanted to own their own homes; in factories where workers felt over-taxed and bullied by union bosses; in small businesses where managers felt their entrepreneurialism was strangled by red tape – in all these places and more there was enthusiastic support for what came to be called Thatcherism. Its symbol was to become the new Georgian-style front door on the streets of so many council estates.

The principal documents that were produced during this period reflected Margaret Thatcher's approach. *The Right Approach* (1976) was deliberately described as a strategy rather than a policy document. It was written to draw together the initial work of the policy groups, setting out general principles of action rather than a detailed plan for government. *The Right Approach to the Economy* (1977) brought together the main policy work that had been done on industrial policy, labour relations, taxation and public expenditure. It also set out a rigorously argued intellectual case for economic reform. Both these documents had to stitch together various shades of opinion in the Party. That was not new. Party policy documents are always part-programme, part-treaty. Particularly in the case of the economic policy there was quite a lot to reconcile! But it was quite elegantly done, with the welcome addition of Angus Maude's pen and those of some other parliamentary colleagues to the usual Research Department draftmanship.

Geoffrey Howe deserves special praise for the role he played in policy-making. He worked very hard; he was on top of the issues; he was unflappably and imperturbably at the heart of many of the most difficult issues, able to bring people together or when necessary simply to tranquilise dissent. He was actually interested in policy and in co-ordinating the work of others to put ideas into sellable and deliverable shape. He deserves considerable credit, in and out of government, for his ability to shape policy.

Just as in 1950 and 1951, when the manifestos were based on the Charters, so in 1978 and 1979 they emerged from the earlier *Right Approach* strategy documents. We anticipated an election in the autumn of 1978, and completed a draft of the manifesto by late summer. Angus Maude and I were in his office in Old Queen Street correcting the page proofs when James Callaghan told the TUC that he was not after all going to call an election before the winter. We could not believe our luck. Perhaps Angus Maude did not quite dance around the huge mahogany table on which the page proofs were laid out, but he came very close to such a breach of public decorum. Analysts of Callaghan's decision would doubtless ascribe some of the cause of his disastrous procrastination to the advertising campaign we had mounted that summer with its very effective Saatchi advertisements featuring dole queues and the famous slogan, 'Labour isn't working'. Nothing should detract from the credit due to the Saatchi team, Tim Bell and Gordon Reece (an insufficiently praised publicist) for the work they did on the presentation of the Party's image. The Research Department worked closely with them. We had very few disagreements. They did a highly effective job, and to be frank we had fun together.

With the election fatally delayed, Angus and I thought that we should flesh out in a little more detail parts of the manifesto. But the leader, some of her colleagues, and events ruled otherwise. Far from lengthening the manifesto, we were instructed to recast it thematically under five main headings – the control of inflation and trade union power; the restoration of incentive; upholding parliament and the rule of law; supporting family life with more efficient welfare services; and strengthening defence. Moreover, we were pressed again and again to cut and shorten the document. At one meeting of the Shadow Cabinet, Peter Thorneycroft argued that the manifesto should be short enough to fit on the back of a postcard 'Why that big?', asked Lord Hailsham. 'Why not a postage stamp?' In the event, we were given a little more space.

The industrial disputes of the winter helped both to determine the manifesto's style and length, but above all to change its content slightly. The outbreak of trade union militancy had begun with squeezing big pay increases out of the Ford Motor Company in breach of the Government's pay policy. In January, strikes spread from road haulage workers to the public sector including the National Health Service. In a very effective Party Political Broadcast in mid-January, in the drafting of which the Research Department was much involved, Margaret Thatcher struck a national rather than a partisan note, offering support for the Government if they were prepared to introduce legislation to ban secondary picketing, to fund strike ballots and to introduce no-strike agreements in essential services.

The industrial chaos, to which the Labour Government appeared to have no response beyond hand-wringing, inevitably led to a strengthening of the manifesto's promises on the trade unions, covering limitations on secondary picketing, the payment of compensation for workers dismissed as a result of a closed shop, and the introduction of postal ballots for union elections. Opinion polls suggested that the Conservative manifesto's proposals were very popular, even though its alleged lack of policy detail and clarity led to Denis Healey saying that looking for policies in it was 'like looking for a black cat in a dark coal cellar.' The electorate evidently disagreed.

*

In the previous chapter, Brendon Sewill makes the point that in 1970 the Conservative Government had a policy on everything except running the economy, and was wrecked on the rocks of events (especially soaring oil prices and the OPEC embargo) with no clear macroeconomic framework for taking decisions. He notes that this was not a failure that could be laid at the door of the CRD since he and others had penned sensible ideas on this subject which had been ignored by Edward Heath and the Party leadership. There was a similar though not exact parallel in the Thatcher years: a policy that was not successfully crafted and presented in Opposition, and that proved disastrous when it came to be fashioned later in government. We called this anti-voter explosive device, the community charge; voters called it the poll tax.

The policy – or at least the demand for any old policy – was born in an argument that Margaret Thatcher sadly lost. In the months between the two 1974 elections, Edward Heath became increasingly convinced (for example by conversations with the Canadian premier, Pierre Trudeau) that the Conservative Government had been ousted in February because it offered voters too bleak and honest a choice. What they demanded were bromides and bribes. The point was not made quite in those terms but that was what was meant. Cynicism should have its day. I was present at a meeting at Heath's house when he pressed Margaret Thatcher again and again as Housing and Local Government Spokesman to accept and make two pledges. The first was to cap mortgages, which had been rising fast, at 9½ per cent. The second was to abolish domestic rates. Thatcher argued strongly that capping mortgages made no economic sense whatever the political attractions; that we should not offer to scrap the existing system of local tax without knowing what we were intending to put in its place; and that in any event to make two implausible pledges doubled the incredibility of what we were offering, so at most we should offer just one electoral bribe, not two. But Heath insisted and won the day. In the subsequent campaign Margaret Thatcher presented both policies brilliantly. At press conferences, none of the justifiably sceptical journalists was able to demolish her arguments. Subsequently, events buried the mortgage cap promise; but the abolition of domestic rating survived as a promise and Margaret Thatcher felt that she had a personal responsibility to deliver on it. In Opposition, in the run-up to the 1979 election, we made no real progress in devising a better system of local taxation, and prevarication on the issue was helped by the publication in 1976 of the Layfield Report on Local

Government Finance, which favoured the retention of domestic and commercial rates.

In government we went around all the familiar arguments about the system. Every new proposal had enough snags and snares to destroy its proponents. So eventually Margaret turned to a group of the cleverest people she could find. The names of the authors of the dreadful idea that emerged from this review are now charitably shrouded in impenetrable mystery, and since some of them are personal friends I should leave them in that obscurity. Enough to say that very clever people are not always equally wise. Whatever its merits in logic, the community charge was a disaster in politics. It homed in like a heat-seeking missile on floating voters in marginal constituencies, precisely the sort of people whom, as I said earlier, Margaret had always understood – along with their purses and pocket-books – so well. I sent Number 10 a careful analysis of this awful truth (not least some prescient calculations by the local government expert Tony Travers) when as Secretary of State for the Environment in 1989 I suddenly found myself handling this hottest of potatoes. How could all this have happened? It was partly that she was determined to honour her earlier pledge on reform; partly that she was distracted by other issues that she thought more important (like her disagreement over Europe with her continental peers and her most important Cabinet colleagues); and partly that she was by then wrapped in that sense of political invincibility that a long tenure in office and the comfort-blanket advice of an inner circle of courtiers and false friends often produces. The meeting at which I discussed with the Prime Minister proposals for mitigating the worst effects of the tax and my worries about its likely consequences was not minuted, or if it was my private office were not sent a copy.

We should make no mistake about it; it was the poll tax that did for her, not Europe or wear-and-tear. The poll tax was the best example I can recall of how not to make policy – the product of intellectual and political hubris, and the end result of a process that began with cynicism and political calculation under Heath and concluded with no sensible political calculation at all under Margaret Thatcher. As I have just noted, even attempts to blunt its worst effects (which admittedly would have destroyed much of its perverse logic) were rejected without the Prime Minister's serious engagement in a political discussion about them.

*

In any period, the Research Department is only as good as the people it recruits and retains – with neither recruitment nor retention owing much to pecuniary motivation. The common room atmosphere – occasionally eccentric, sometimes in the 1970s even a tad louche – is captured with only a little exaggeration in Matthew Parris's memoirs, *Chance Witness: An Outsider's Life in Politics*. There were several stars, some of whom went on to assume the status commonly assigned to heavenly bodies. Others laboured mightily and effectively beyond the limelight. One or two added to the collective geniality without doing much harm to anyone including the Labour Government.

This is no headmaster's prize-giving report, so there will be no naming of names save to say that those whom Margaret Thatcher saw most frequently like Adam Ridley, Stephen Sherbourne, Matthew Parris, Michael Dobbs, Dermot Gleeson and Nick True appeared to earn her trust and she earned their admiration, shot through from time to time with both affection and astonishment. But altogether, the Research Department – 'a good little destroyer', as Michael Fraser once called it – did more than might reasonably have been expected of such a modestly endowed operation to help win the 1979 election, a victory which was secured above all by Margaret Thatcher's courage, vision and élan and by the Labour Government's political bankruptcy.

David Cameron
TRADITION AND CHANGE

DAVID CAMERON joined the Conservative Research Department in September 1988. He covered trade, industry and energy issues in the Economics Section before moving to the Political Section, of which he became Head in 1990. He left the Department after the 1992 election on his appointment as Special Adviser to the Chancellor of the Exchequer. He was elected Leader of the Conservative Party in December 2005.

EDITOR'S NOTE: The essays in this volume concentrate largely on the work done by the Research Department during periods in opposition to help restore the Party to power. Here the most distinguished of the CRD's graduates of the last twenty years reflects on the role of the Department during a momentous period of Conservative Government, and on the changes initiated then to modernise its organisation for a fast-moving political world.

John Wyndham carved out a special niche for himself as Private Secretary to Harold Macmillan. But he worked for a time in CRD, joining after the war. And talking about his time there he remarked that what he liked about the Department was its 'bohemian sort of efficiency.'[1] Even by the late 1980s, it was a description I could recognise. I will always associate CRD with an ordered sort of chaos. Papers on the floor, rather than in files. Lunches that went on for considerably longer than would seem appropriate today. Deadlines met, only just. My time there taught me the most important lesson I have ever learned about politics – it may be a serious business, but it should never be stuffy or dull.

It certainly seemed serious when I first walked through the door. I'll always remember Alistair Cooke, the Deputy Director, letting me know exactly what was expected of me:

'Mr Cameron, all your drafts for briefing papers and speeches must be written with absolute clarity; they must be set properly in the context of Mrs Thatcher's evolving programme of reform; they must give accurate sources for all references; and they must draw out the weak points in the Opposition's policies. Jargon is absolutely forbidden.'

But when you peeled away the old-fashioned formality of CRD's stalwarts, what lurked underneath was a group of people with brains, wit, a love of politics and a simple determination to preserve the high standards of CRD – standards without which it would not enjoy Margaret Thatcher's confidence. And their methods worked. As the Party was in Government at the time, policy was largely outside our domain; but we were responsible for providing the key facts and information that Ministers and MPs relied on to back up their arguments and promote new legislation in Parliament, reinforced by a thorough analysis of the Opposition's policies. For those of us involved in preparing the material, the work was rigorous. But, when you heard your material being used by a Minister on television or in the chamber of the House of Commons, it was extremely rewarding.

The formality of my bosses at CRD contrasted sharply with the informality found elsewhere. One of the best things about CRD is that it puts fresh-faced graduates at the side of senior members of the Party within moments of their arrival. At twenty-one, I found myself briefing Trade, Industry and Energy Ministers, almost from the first day, as well as the MPs who attended the specialist backbench committees covering those subjects. And they were easier to get on with than you would think. DTI morning meetings were always interesting, with Ministers taking it in turns to have a go at each other. 'My constituents are furious with the Government', said one. 'Serves you right for going to your constituency', replied Alan Clark.

One person whom I got on with well was the Party Chairman, Chris Patten, who taught me the art of writing a decent speech. The skills I picked up from him, the training I got in preparing briefing material from the Director of CRD, Robin Harris, and the lectures from that legendary grammarian, Alistair Cooke, all stood me in good stead for the future. One particularly fond memory is coming into contact with that great man and outstanding patriot, Ian Gow. In 1989, in the frenzied atmosphere after the fall of the Berlin Wall, I helped him prepare for a debate in the House of Commons on the new opportunities for mankind. After it was over, he rewarded me with the ultimate accolade: two of his famous white lady cocktails in the Pugin Room of the House of Commons. It was a gesture that made a lasting impression on a twenty-something researcher. Like so many others, I mourned Ian Gow when he was murdered by IRA terrorists a year later. I felt honoured and privileged to have done a small piece of work for him.

Of course, during my time at CRD the most senior figure of all was Mrs Thatcher. I'll never forget my first meeting with her. Walking around at an office party, she stopped in front of me and asked: 'What are the trade figures? Have you seen the trade figures today?' I had not. She had. I never made the same mistake again.

When this happened, Britain's greatest peace-time Prime Minister was in her third term. Her first two terms focused on radical economic change, so now the time had come to address issues that had been previously been neglected. Chief amongst them was local government finance and what came to be her nemesis, the poll tax. It is too often overlooked that her powerful statements on global warming [2] were far ahead of her time. And it was during this period that she began to develop her programme for public service reform by freeing schools and hospitals from the dead hand of bureaucratic control and advancing parental and patient choice.

I remember thinking back then that we should have gone much further, much earlier, in giving people more power and control over public services and their personal lives, as we had done in their economic lives. Just as tax reduction and trade union reform took time to bed down and become irreversible, so too do reforms of public services. The strong vein of social Conservatism which runs through our history – as the first essays in this volume demonstrate – was not given as much prominence as perhaps it should have been.

Even so, the changes that were made to the public services meant that after Mrs Thatcher had gone, John Major regularly faced attacks from an unreconstructed Labour Party during Prime Minister's Questions. By then I was the head of CRD's Political Section, so it was my responsibility to help provide ammunition for those encounters. I quickly learnt that on health, Labour would stop at nothing in their attacks. They sank to new depths in 1991, when at their Party Conference Neil Kinnock claimed 'the Tories will privatise the National Health Service'. This set the seal on what I labelled as 'Labour's unforgivable campaign on health' in the chapter analysing their policies published in *The Campaign Guide 1992*.

Learning vital skills such as briefing and speech-writing; ready access to the Party's senior figures; providing the material to counter attacks on our policies; above all, being serious, but enjoying politics: I'd like to think that those working in CRD today are having the same, and invaluable, experience I had back then. After all, tradition matters, particularly to Tories. But that doesn't mean nothing has changed.

When I joined the Department, nearly ten years had passed since it had left its original, and much treasured, home in Old Queen Street and moved into Smith Square to join the other Departments of Central Office. Yet it still managed to avoid having too much to do with them. In my time all that began to change, as it had to. I tried to make myself useful to the Campaigning Department by contributing to their leaflets, working with them closely during the Vauxhall by-election of June 1989. And as Head of Political Section, I also worked closely with the Press Office.

This was the beginning of a profound culture change for CRD, moving towards the integration of the key Departments so they could work together as a single team. Today all the old barriers to effective co-operation with other Departments have been swept away and CRD forms part of a wider united team at Conservative Campaign Headquarters. But even in an open-plan office, CRD retains its own unique character under its current Director, James O'Shaughnessy, as he makes clear in his contribution to this volume.

It has not sacrificed its old traditions or *esprit de corps*. But it has acquired new working methods needed to be really effective in the fast-moving political world of 2009.

I think the balance is right. There were some aspects of life in CRD as I encountered it in 1988 which had to change. We had to make it more open, faster on its feet and better able to work with the rest of the professional Party machine. But there were some incredibly valuable things that needed to stay the same: well-researched policy papers, well-argued speech drafts, banks of accurate facts and quotes, and of course *The Campaign Guide*. Our tradition of CRD rigour continues to supply all these. Politicians learn their craft in different ways. I am glad I learnt mine the CRD way.

Notes

[1] Lord Egremont, *Wyndham and Children First* (Macmillan, 1968), p. 141.

[2] Her speeches were edited and printed by Alistair Cooke in a pamphlet, *Our Threatened Environment: The Conservative Response* (Conservative Political Centre, 1990).

James O'Shaughnessy
CRD UNDER CAMERON

JAMES O'SHAUGHNESSY joined the Department in June 2001. He dealt initially with work and pensions issues, and then education and skills until June 2003. He returned as Director in September 2007.

The history of the CRD, so evocatively described in the earlier essays in this book, has been unusually volatile in recent years, not least because Oliver Letwin's partial allusion to Voltaire – if the CRD did not exist it would have been necessary for the Party to invent it – has been tested to destruction by the reconstitution of the Department, not once, but twice since 2001. It is not hard to see why these upheavals happened. The lean earlier years of our long spell in Opposition put immense pressure on departmental budgets, and also made it difficult to prevent a note of rather weary scepticism creeping into the minds of desk officers. This was not exactly conducive to fostering a winning mentality, something I can attest to from my first spell in CRD as a humble desk officer between 2001 and 2003 when, despite genuine efforts to develop a new and more compassionate brand of Conservatism, very little seemed to go our way. Opposition can indeed be miserable, and many of us have known nothing else, but misery cannot be allowed to fester.

The Department, like the Party itself, bounced back. Restored to vigorous life by Michael Howard with Greg Clark as Director, it worked closely with him and his team before, and during, the 2005 election. It is today playing a central part in David Cameron's preparations for the next election. John Glen, as Director in 2005-6, contributed notably to the greater stability that now exists. The Department endures not only, I believe, because it fulfils a function that is always required by a modern political Party, but because it fulfils that function better than any other body could do. In this short essay I will explain a little about how the research and policy functions of the Party operate under David Cameron's leadership. Readers who may be hoping for fireworks must excuse the lack of insider gossip and stories. Now is not the time for them. They will have to wait for (much) later editions of this book.

Probably the defining feature of the CRD in the first couple of years of David Cameron's leadership was its concentration on policy, a fact closely bound up with Oliver Letwin's simultaneous appointment at the end of 2005 as Chairman of both the CRD and David's very detailed Policy Review. While the usual functions associated with the CRD of the post-war era – political research, analysis and briefing – continued to be carried out by desk officers and the sharp minds of the Political Section (then, as now, under the astute leadership of Oliver Dowden), the scale of resources focused on the Policy Review – undoubtedly the biggest wholesale review of the Party's policy for thirty years – was remarkable.

There were six main policy groups. They looked in great depth and openness of mind at economic competitiveness, national and international security, globalisation and global poverty, quality of life, public services and social justice. Each group, headed by a senior Conservative politician and an experienced and independent expert, was serviced by at least one full-time member of staff , often assisted by the relevant desk officer and other staff where appropriate. In addition, dozens of task forces, special groups, commissions and other bodies were set up to undertake the colossal task of re-evaluating Conservative Party policy from the bottom up, all with at least some assistance from the CRD.

As well as recognising this once in a generation endeavour for what it was, it is important to bear in mind the political value of the exercise (and therefore the justification for the involvement of the CRD). The Policy Review not only created a new policy platform for the leadership to build on; it also demonstrated to the media, to all those with a deep interest in politics, and, most importantly, to voters at large, that the Conservative Party was once again keen to hear what the outside world had to say. As Michael Ashcroft's famous analysis *Smell the Coffee* (2005) had shown, during the previous decade many voters had simply abandoned any hope that the Conservative Party might share their values or want to understand their lives. The Policy Review process might have been messy at times, as all large exercises of this kind in democratic power-sharing are likely to be, but it provided irrefutable evidence that the Party was trying to reconnect with the British people once again.

Beyond that, it was both a concrete demonstration of the political values which David Cameron has put at the heart of today's Conservative Party – the twin ideas that politicians don't have all the answers and that open, fully accountable, wiki-style, post-bureaucratic government is the most suitable and effective for the twenty-first century – and a very successful exercise in binding the broad Conservative family together, and renewing its appetite for power.

*

I rejoined the CRD as Director in September 2007, just as the Policy Review came to its official end and the Party was gearing up for the expected general election in October or November that year. Our Party Conference at Blackpool in 2007 was of course a major turning-point. One thing that few people have commented on is how the process of the Policy Review actually helped that remarkable event to be the success that it was. Policy was at the heart of our Blackpool fightback, most famously with George Osborne's announcement on lifting the inheritance tax threshold. But the success of the Review meant that we now had the ideas to match the changing perception of the Party, as well as the unity to feel confident that the Party as a whole would row in behind these new ideas.

Despite David Cameron's unforgettable and game-changing speech, we were still preparing for the election until the last possible minute. My own post-Conference Saturday was spent editing the manifesto, put together by Oliver Letwin and the Shadow Cabinet over the preceding summer, with short breaks to watch England beating Australia in the Rugby World Cup. As news filtered through that day that Brown had 'bottled' the election, we all felt disappointment that we were being denied the chance to persuade the country to vote for change. Once that disappointment faded, however, there was quiet optimism about this unexpected opportunity to develop our political programme further.

By this stage the desk officers – now called special advisers – had been brought back together again within Conservative Campaign Headquarters, after a period during which many of them had been dispersed around the offices of the Shadow Cabinet, and the CRD re-emerged in its current form. I began to reshape the Department into discrete sections – now co-located with their press officers in order to hone the results of our work and break down the traditional divide between press and research – to ensure effective management of the Department and to provide opportunities for more experienced staff to advance their careers (both features sorely lacking in the 'flat' structures of the Department in the recent past). In a Department now employing around twenty special advisers, we have Foreign Affairs, Home Affairs, Public Services, Economic Competitiveness and Briefing Sections, each headed by a senior special adviser. There is a separate Treasury team – a hybrid research, policy and press section of eight advisers – located in George Osborne's Private Office. These changes have, I hope, built up some team solidarity as well as giving special advisers the chance to develop a wider knowledge base through exposure to different but similar briefs within their sections. The CRD is now managed with skill by my Deputy for research, Nick Timothy.

My first instruction to the team on rejoining the reconstructed Department was that we needed to relearn the importance of using the media to hold the Government to account. It is a truth in politics that every Government is subject to the natural wear and tear that comes from simply being in power, but as we ourselves have discovered it is possible for a disintegrating administration to rage against the dying of the light for much longer than most people would imagine. Political gravity is not a constant force; it can be weakened or strengthened by the actions of the Opposition Parties. For a Department like the CRD in the modern political era, this means that it is not enough merely to provide analysis, briefing and research. In Opposition it also has to concentrate on discovering and deploying information that hastens the end of a sitting Government by demonstrating that it is losing both its ability to govern and its empathy with voters.

Using a range of tools, from tried and trusted research methods like Parliamentary written questions through to newer techniques like web searches and freedom of information requests, the CRD today is – at times – as brilliant at investigative journalism as any occupant of the Lobby. Whether exposing the Government's secret plans to impose a 'tax on nice homes', showing how thousands of prisoners have been released before their time is up, demonstrating that we have been slipping down the international school league tables, or explaining why a local GP surgery is threatened with closure, an essential part of our armoury these days is the research-driven story that destroys the Government's claims to competence. Members of CRD are now expected to deliver high profile media stories, which they do with amazing regularity. Next time you see a news story showing how the Labour Government is failing in some way, there is a good chance it will be one of ours. Of course this isn't enough to win a general election campaign, far from it, but it is a prerequisite for victory that any Opposition Party ignores at its peril.

*

If Opposition is in part about winning over voters while undermining the claims of the Government of the day, launching new policy proposals is of course the other essential weapon in the armoury. What we have attempted to do during the last few years is to use policy-making in a dual role – first, to prepare a platform for government should we be fortunate enough to win the next general election; and second, to help us express our values and influence the media coverage of the Party.

Written like that it sounds simple, and it seems obvious that these goals should be not just be compatible but completely coterminous. But in reality there is always the risk that short-term demands will contaminate long-term goals, as well as the opposite risk that the fundamentally drawn-out nature of good policy-making can leave us leaden-footed and exposed to the rapidly changing nature of modern political life. Anyone familiar with the day-to-day operation of politics will know just how powerful is the effect of the news cycle, and the premium attached to being able to bend it at least a little to your will. The challenge is to do so in such a way that policy is not compromised.

Ultimately, of course, winning comes from presenting a positive, coherent, well-researched programme rooted in a vision of the better world that one wants to create. Over the past two years we have used the medium of 'Green Papers' – consultative policy papers that are much like Government White Papers in form – as the main vehicles for communicating the ideas through which we want to change Britain. We have built up, from scratch, a Policy Unit of eight experts drawn from academia, the civil service, business and think-tanks. Led shrewdly by my Deputy for policy, Sean Worth, the Unit is responsible for doing most of the preparatory work for the 'Green Papers' and other, mainly domestic policy proposals that the Party publishes (the Treasury team retains the policy-making function for most economic, financial and fiscal matters).

The activities of the Policy Unit, working hand-in-glove with the Party leadership and the Shadow Cabinet as a whole, have covered the main areas of domestic policy, from schools and the NHS to prisons and the environment, but have also been driven by the amazing series of crises that have affected Britain in the last two years – from the slow-burn of widespread social breakdown, via the existential emergency of the economic crisis, to the paradigm-shifting expenses scandal from which British politics has barely started to recover.

Out of these developments has emerged a new political philosophy, or at least a new configuration of established theories and values, which we call progressive Conservatism. This is the idea that the progressive aims of fairness, security, opportunity and sustainability can only be successfully pursued through the Conservative means of strengthening society, decentralising power and rebuilding a diversified economy. As the CRD has helped to demonstrate over the last few years, Labour have comprehensively failed to deliver these goals. Our policy programme, on which the manifesto will be based, shows how the next Conservative Government will make good its promise of a better Britain, even against the terrible fiscal backdrop we will inherit if we win. And if we do win, then CRD will once again have been at the heart of victory.

Michael Dobbs
CONCLUSION: AN EXTRAORDINARY POLITICAL BACKROOM

MICHAEL DOBBS worked in the Research Department from 1975 until 1979. He subsequently became Chief of Staff and later Deputy Chairman of the Conservative Party, as well as being Deputy Chairman of the Party's advertising agency, Saatchi & Saatchi. He is now a novelist, his works including a series of four novels about Winston Churchill.

The Conservative Research Department has always been more than simply an organisation. From its foundation eight decades ago, its story has not been about bureaucracy but about extraordinary men and women. That is what has made it so much fun.

Yet it has never been flippant. There is an enduring magic about the Department, so well captured in these essays, that has enabled it to take mostly callow young men and women from assorted backgrounds, paying them wages that elsewhere would be regarded as a gross insult, and transforming them into a hugely successful political war machine.

My own introduction during the 1970s was entirely typical, in the sense that there is no mould into which a CRD officer (or special adviser, as he or she is now known) must fit. I had wandered into 24 Old Queen Street in jeans and a ragged student sweatshirt in search of political leaflets; I somehow ended up in the office of a jolly and rather portly man dressed in a chalk-stripe three-piece suit who appeared to be trying to coax his brains out through his ear with the encouragement of a letter opener. He looked at my attire with intense suspicion. 'Why do you want to work here?' he demanded in a squeaky voice, clearly under the impression that I was a fully fledged member of Militant.

'I don't,' I blurted in surprise.

'Why not? This is a most wonderful place to work. Are you looking for a job?'

'Well, I might be, in a few months. When I finish graduate school …'

So began a most unconventional job interview. James Douglas, the Director and my unintended host, gave me a two-hour lecture on the attractions of the Department while he filled out my job application form. I stumbled from his office bemused but inspired, not quite understanding what I had let myself in for. I suspect the Party didn't, either.

As Oliver Letwin points out in his introduction, political Parties are rarely giants of intellectual originality, but ideas are their primary weapons. The great game is based on the clash of ideas, a confrontation between different perspectives, and when Parties lose their sense of purpose, they lose their way and are condemned to electoral oblivion. It is a hugely painful but entirely necessary part of the process of political renewal and it is when the going is at its toughest, in Opposition, that the Research Department really comes into its own. Reading through the reflections in these essays, that process of renewal is what the Research Department has been engaged in ever since its formation. As Alistair Cooke recounts, Neville Chamberlain started it, declaring that his prime objective was to 'do something to improve the condition for the less fortunate classes'. In 1929, without power but with reforming passion, he needed support and resources. So the Conservative Research Department was born.

Yet we shouldn't be too high-minded; politics are, after all, a tooth and claw affair. One of Chamberlain's closest associates was Major Joseph Ball. I first came across his name through his role as an enthusiastic advocate of the dark arts, an enforcer for Neville Chamberlain who was reputed to have burgled the homes of MPs and tapped the telephones of most of the Cabinet. He also paid someone inside Odhams Printers, the main supplier to the Labour Party, so ensuring that the first copy of Labour's Manifesto ended up not at Transport House but with him. Yet this was also the man who became the first

Director of the Research Department. He was a man for all seasons, and most particularly for long wintry nights. I am glad that Alistair Cooke now plans to give us the full story of this Prince of Darkness.

CRD has never been an ivory tower. During its eight decades it has been central to some of the seminal events of the age – before the war helping launch ground-breaking initiatives on regional policy and the coal industry, and after it moving forward the house-building boom that made Harold Macmillan's reputation. I was surprised and amused by Brendon Sewill's recollection that the Research Department discovered monetarism even before Margaret Thatcher stumbled across it. These triumphs were far from inevitable, and were certainly not conceived in comfort.

The hardy folk who have sustained the Research Department never did so for material reward – almost every essay in this work records hours and conditions that would have made nonsense of any number of EU directives. Our labour was often sweated, and getting stuck in the ancient lift in Old Queen Street was an occupational hazard – as was falling in love. Enoch and Pam Powell's was but one of many happy marriages that have been forged in the dusty corners and pursued within the filing cupboards of the Research Department, perhaps in the hope that poverty shared might turn out to be poverty halved. No one ever worked there because of the money.

What has drawn so many exceptional men and women to the Department over the years was not financial returns but what could be achieved there – and not just for themselves, although ambition has always been part of its appeal. It has been a superb training ground for political leaders who emerged from the back room, like Macleod, Maudling, Hurd, Powell, Patten, Portillo and the rest – although Westminster is a serendipitous world, and among the applicants who were turned down by the Research Department were Guy Burgess and Ted Heath. Alongside the great names have been many others who simply wanted to play their part, attracted by its 'bohemian sort of efficiency', to which David Cameron refers, and not unduly worried about the fire hazard presented by so much ill-sorted paper.

I never made history while I was there, but I was part of it. The title given to me by Chris Patten was that of Special Duties Officer. In this age of renditions and grey wars, such an ambiguous title has a sinister ring to it, but my job definition was simple: 'Keep Margaret happy'. I was assigned to her service during a time in Opposition when the crucible of history glowed with extraordinary heat. The country was in chaos, some claimed it was ungovernable, others even predicted a Marxist takeover. Yes, it was that bad.

My duties at that time included acting as secretary to what we loosely named the 'Muck-Up Squad', a group of backbenchers, led by the impeccably polite Sir Jasper More and corralled by the equally impeccably dressed Deputy Chief Whip, Jack Weatherill. The group's purpose was simple, to hound and harass the Callaghan Government around the floor of the House of Commons until it was worn down. This was pursued using statistics and details of the Government's failings, extracted like rotten teeth from the jaws of reluctant Ministries through the persistent questioning of CRD officers. It was a huge success. Joseph Ball would have been proud.

Eventually the Callaghan Government was brought low, not just by their paymasters in the trade unions but also through ferocious Parliamentary activity, a mixture of pointed questioning and focused debate which was succoured by the Research Department. Such great events are not originated by research officers, but they are brought to more glorious life by them. And in turn they give those officers a ringside seat on great times. I was the first person on that extraordinary election night in 1979 to be able to tell Margaret she had won. If service to her was sometimes a bumpy road, it was never a dull one.

In the aftermath of that victory, Margaret decreed that the Research Department should lose its fiefdom in Old Queen Street and be amalgamated with Party headquarters. I was never a fan of such a move, but in my final few weeks there I was instructed by the new Director, Alan Howarth (a most genial but distracted man who has ended up on the Labour benches in the House of Lords, following in the footsteps of one of CRD's founder members, Lord Longford) to make suitable arrangements for the transfer to Smith Square. I live in shame that my incompetence delayed the move by many months. Despite Chris Patten's typically gracious remarks about Margaret, there were many hurt feelings about the turn of events after such a prodigious effort. She was always a woman in a hurry.

Yet the move was not only financially inevitable but almost certainly desirable. The art of politics was changing. It was once said of Rab Butler that he was the only man in the country who could stretch a partridge to six; the meat of modern politics allows for much less delicate carving. It was inescapable that the idea and the message should be brought closer together, that the fighting machine should be able to move more rapidly and fire more frequently. As James O'Shaughnessy outlines, this has been achieved in organisational terms, and it should not be forgotten that Joseph Ball was not only CRD Director but also Director of Publicity at CCO. A Party that can sit at the same table as its principles is always stronger than one that has forgotten why it accepted the invitation to dine in the first place.

Even as it adapts to new challenges, it is tradition, continuity and coherence that lie at the heart of successful Conservatism, and for the last 80 years the Research Department has been the custodian of that process. We have come a long way from the modest origins of the 1930s, through the social earnestness of the 1950s and the 'policy-wonkery' of the 1970s and 80s to the 'wiki-ways' of the new millennium. It has been a voyage of high adventure undertaken by extraordinarily talented and mostly young men and women. The Department has always taken its peculiar mixture of enthusiasm, expertise and ambition and made itself so much more than the sum of the parts.

The forthcoming general election will usher in a new era for the Research Department, because it will not only be at the heart of the campaign but also at its head. It is perhaps something of a surprise, given the quality and stellar careers of so many CRD graduates, that David Cameron is the first Party leader to have emerged from its training ground, but there is always new ground to break. His career is a fitting tribute to the Department's exceptional achievements. It is also a mark of its continuing relevance.

APPENDIX 1

CHAIRMEN AND DIRECTORS OF THE CONSERVATIVE RESEARCH DEPARTMENT

Chairmen:

1930–40	Neville Chamberlain
1940–43	Sir Kingsley Wood
1943–45	Sir Joseph Ball*
1945–64	R. A. Butler
1964–70	*post vacant*
1970–74	Sir Michael (later Lord) Fraser
1974–75	Sir Ian Gilmour
1975–79	Angus Maude
1979–97	*post abolished and functions assumed by Party Chairman*
1997	David Willetts
1997–2003	*post vacant*
2003–04	David Willetts
2004–05	George Bridges
2005–	Oliver Letwin

Directors:

1930–39	Sir Joseph Ball
1939–45	*post vacant*
1945–51	David Clarke
1948–50	Henry Hopkinson†
1948–59	Percy Cohen†

1951–64	Michael Fraser
1964–70	Brendon Sewill
1970–74	James Douglas
1974–79	Chris Patten
1979–82	Alan Howarth
1982–84	Peter Cropper
1985–89	Robin Harris
1990–95	Andrew Lansley
1995–98	Daniel Finkelstein
1999–2003	Rick Nye
2003–05	Greg Clark
2005–06	John Glen
2006–07	George Bridges‡
2007–	James O'Shaughnessy

The following have held the post briefly: Adam Ridley (1979 election), Dermot Gleeson (after 1979 election) and Alistair Cooke (Acting Director, 1984–5 and 1989–90).

---

* Acting Chairman.
† Jointly.
‡ Styled Political Director.

APPENDIX 2

THE RECORDS OF THE CONSERVATIVE RESEARCH DEPARTMENT

The extensive records of the Conservative Research Department, housed in some 1,480 boxes, which go back to its inception in 1929, are held in the Conservative Party Archive at the Bodleian Library in Oxford. They form perhaps the most important of the various collections held in the Archive, not least because they survived the depredations of war, salvage drives and administrative disinterest virtually intact, unlike those of the pre-war Conservative Central Office.

The central role it assumed in the Party's policy-making process meant that CRD officers researched a wide range of issues for the Party Leader, serviced Committees of the Parliamentary Party from the Shadow Cabinet downwards, provided authoritative briefs to MPs in preparation for Parliamentary debates, played a major role in the writing of Party publications and the vetting of Party publicity, and analysed public opinion trends in order to advise the leadership on electoral strategy. One of the most significant aspects of the records it left behind results from its pivotal role in the major exercises of policy renewal undertaken by the Party during prolonged periods of opposition. It was prolific in the number of detailed reports and papers it turned out in these periods, particularly during 1945-51, 1964-1970 and, more recently, 2005-07.

The majority of its papers from 1929 until the mid-1970s have already been catalogued and made available to researchers. The first two essays in this volume draw on the CRD papers up to 1951. (Papers in the personal possession of Brendon Sewill, CRD Director between 1964 and 1970, form the basis of his essay.) Work has recently begun to provide access to over 900 additional boxes of papers of CRD papers held at the Bodleian which date from the mid-1960s to the 1990s which, when finished, will nearly treble the amount of material now available, and hopefully lead to further fresh insights and new appraisals of the work of the Department and the contribution it has made over the past eighty years.

JEREMY McILWAINE

Conservative Party Archivist

Index

A
Advisory Committee on Policy
    under Butler, 42
        :Heath, 55, 58
        :Thatcher, 83, 86

Agricultural policy, 21, 42

Amery, Leo
    need for Conservative policy work, 8

B
Baldwin, Stanley
    improved diet for British families, 20
    Party crisis after 1929, 15-16
    origins of CRD, 8-9
    relations with Neville Chamberlain, 6
    view of policy-making, 7-8

Ball, Joseph
    Chamberlain's 'enforcer', 108-9
    imperial preference, 17-18
    man of secrets, 10-11
    new programme of work for CRD, 19
    Ottawa Conference, 18
    physical fitness campaign, 19, 20-21
    superb CRD Director, 11, 23
    war-time CRD guardian, 29

Bell, Tim, 89

Bellairs, Charles, 57
    work with Thatcher, 79

Boswell, Tim
    CRD booklet, 65

Bow Group, 2

Boyle, Sir Edward, 56, 79

Branston, Ursuala
    charm of CRD, 37
    Eden's wrath, 37

Briggs, Elizabeth (now Buchanan)
    CRD agriculture expert, 37

Brooke, Henry
    anonymous articles in *The Times*, 13
    Chamberlain's man, 12, 23
    founder member of CRD, 12
    imperial preference, 17
    in Parliament, 13, 23
    linchpin of CRD, 13, 21, 29
    Tariff Committee, 16

Buchan, John
    need for political research work, 8

Burgess, Guy
    applicant for CRD post, 109-10

Butler, R. A.,
    as a writer, 36
    assessment of 1951 victory, 50
    Conservatism and, 39-40
    credentials as CRD Chairman, 30
    deep interest in CRD, 31
    famous Rabism on M.Fraser, 38n
    fleeting CRD appearances in later career, 55
    'his best chance' of becoming PM, 47-8
    Industrial Charter, 40-1, 49
    on Thatcher, 82-3
    'pink socialism', 41, 47
    post-war Conservative revival, 38-43
    praise for, 31, 47
    Right Road for Britain, 43-4

C

Cameron, David, 88
    CRD under his leadership, 101-6
    first meeting with Margaret Thatcher, 97
    first Party leader from CRD, 112
    his work in CRD, 95-9
    policy review, 102-3
    public service reform, 97-8

Campaign Guide
    pre-war, 15, 57
    post-war, 44, 57, 98, 99

Carr, Robert, 81

Centre for Policy Studies
    relationship with CRD, 85

Chamberlain, Neville,
    Chairman of CRD, 9-10, 17, 19-24
    Chief Tory policy-maker, 7-8
    CRD's role, 9-10, 14
    national health services, 20-1
    physical fitness campaign, 21
    praised by Butler, 22
    reputation of, 5-7
    social reform, 6,23
    tariff reform, 16-17

Channon, 'Chips'.
    candidates who 'could not even read', 15n

Churchill, Winston
    escapes Butler challenge for premiership, 47-8
    his post-war CRD reconstruction plan thwarted, 29
    ignores Salford letter, 28
    manifesto for 1950 election, 44
    opposed to detailed policy-making, 40
    post-war policy documents, 41, 43-4
    relations with Butler, 48

Clark, Alan, 96

Clark, Greg
    CRD Director, 101

Clarke, David
    arrival at CRD, 13
    'a true intellectual', 32
    CRD Director, 31, 32-3, 35, 40, 42, 43-4
    imperial preference, 18
    post-war Conservative revival, 32
    1939 draft election manifesto, 22-3
    1950 manifesto, 44

Coal industry
    CRD proposals, 19

Cobden Turner, H.
    sums up post-war Tory predicament, 27

Cohen, Percy
    CRD joint Director, 32

Conservative Parliamentary Secretariat, 33, 48

Conservative Party policy
    Cameron's policy review, 102-3
    continuity after the war, 42, 47

    Heath's policy review, 58-62
    free market, 41, 84
    issues in the 1970s, 81-92
    role of the state, 21-2, 47
    Thatcher's caution, 84
    welfare state, 23, 34, 61-2

Conservative Political Centre (CPC)
    role in political education, 12

Conservative Research Department (CRD)
    assessment of its post-war role, 47-50
    briefing for election candidates, 15, 44, 57
    character of, 1-4, 14, 95-6, 98-9, 107-8, 109-10, 111-12
    Chairmen and Directors, 113
    Charters, 40-2
    cost of, 30n
    failure on property-owning democracy, 49
    foundation of, 8-9
    housing policy after the war, 45-6
    importance of secretaries, 31-2, 65
    its work in the 1930s, 15-23
        :after the war, 29-30
        :under Cameron,101-6
        :under Heath, 55-77
        :under Thatcher, 82-90
    move to Smith Square, 98, 110-11
    recent history of, 101-5
    reintroduction of tariffs,16-17
    relations with CPS, 85-6
    policy review under Cameron, 101-7
    post-war work,
        :continuity, 22, 47
        :golden era?, 47-50
    records of, 115
    size and organisation in the late 1960s, 56-8
    size pre-war, 10
        :post-war, 31
    state and industry 21-2, 47
    under Thatcher, 82-90
    women in, 37

Cooke, Alistair
    CRD Deputy Director, 95-6

Cope, John
    assists Heath on Finance Bill, 67

Cosgrave, Patrick,
    anti-Heath, 68

Cropper, Peter
    CRD does not do research, 1

Cunliffe-Lister, Philip
    Tariff Committee, 17

D

Davidson, J. C. C.
    establishment of CRD, 8

Dean, Paul,
    future of social services, 61

Dobbs, Michael
    character of CRD, 107-10, 111-12
    role in CRD, 110-11

Douglas, James
    'academic and absent-minded' Director, 58, 60
    eccentric interviewer, 107-8

Douglas-Home, Sir Alec
    Scottish policy group, 60

Dowden, Oliver, 102

E

Economic policy,
    comes 'unstuck' under Heath, 71-7
    inflation, 73-6
    under Thatcher, 84, 88

Eden, Anthony
    irritated by praise of Butler, 47
    preparation of *Right Road for Britain*, 43
    property-owning democracy, 49
    throws book at CRD officer, 37

Election manifestos
    1935 manifesto, 21
    1939 draft, 22-3
    1950 manifesto, 44-5
    1966 manifesto, 59
    1974 October, 81
    1979 manifesto, 89-90

European Economic Community
    Conservative difficulties, 63
    policy in the late 1960s, 70-1
    Thatcher's approach in opposition, 87

F
Fisher, Warren
    praises Chamberlain, 6

Foreign policy
    CRD's work in the late 1960s, 59-60, 63

Fraser, Michael
    assessment of post-war CRD, 42
    backroom boys dictum, 85
    Charters, 40, 42
    CRD Director, 32, 36, 37
    Deputy Chairman of the Party, 57
    famous Rabism, 38n
    friendship with Heath, 32
    Party's 'best adjutant', 36
    praise for Butler, 47
    trusted adviser of successive leaders, 38n

G
Gilmour, Ian
    October 1974 election manifesto, 81
    replaced as CRD Chairman, 83

Gleeson, Dermot, 93

Glen, John
    CRD Director, 101

Gow, Ian
    assisted by David Cameron, 97

Goldman, Peter
    CRD role, 36-7
    Orpington by-election, 36
    report on Scotland, 60
    value to Butler, 36

Greenland, Tony, 57
    view of Thatcher, 79-80

H
Harris, Robin
    CRD Director, 96

Hayhoe, Barney
    reform of family allowances, 62

Heath, Edward
    character of, 56, 59, 74, 82
    'cost of living proposals', 72-3

  denationalisation proposals, 61
  Europe, 63, 70-1, 75-6
  failure of his Government, 69-77
  friendship with M. Fraser, 32
  ignores inflation dangers, 74-6
  insists domestic rates must be replaced, 91
  takes charge of policy, 55
  unsuccessful CRD applicant, 32-3
  wealth tax proposals, 60-1

Health
  Chamberlain's commitment to, 20
  NHS, 44-5

Hodgson, Patricia
  broadcasting desk officer, 67

Hogg, Quintin
  Case for Conservatism, 39
  draftsman of policy document, 43
  trade union reform, 70
  1979 manifesto, 90

Hopkinson, Henry
  CRD joint Director, 32, 43

Housing
  key area of post-war policy work, 45-6

Howard, Michael
  revival of CRD, 101

Howarth, Alan
  CRD Director and Labour Minister, 111

Howe, Sir Geoffrey
  reconstruction of economic policy, 89

Howell, David
  machinery of government proposals, 70

Hudson, Miles
  takes Lord Carrington to Biafra, 66

Hurd, Douglas
  role in CRD, 65

I
Imperial preference, 17-19

Industrial Charter, 40-2

J

Johnson, Stanley
    as MEP, 67
    pioneering work on the environment, 67

Jones, Thomas
    unimpressed by CRD's start, 9

Joseph, Sir Keith
    Centre for Policy Studies, 83
    policy work before 1979, 83-4, 85

K

Kinnock, Neil
    Tories 'will privatise the NHS', 98

L

Lamont, Norman
    CRD appointment, 67
    Social Priorities Working Group, 61

Letwin, Oliver
    character of CRD, 1-4
    policy review under Cameron, 102

Lewis, Avis
    fear of, 31
    'indomitable personnel officer', 65
    match-making, 32

Longford, 7th Earl of
    founder member of CRD, 11
    idealism of, 11-12
    political education scheme, 12

M

MacDonald, Ramsay, 12

MacGregor, John
    Head of Heath's Private Office, 66

Macleod, Iain
    biography of Chamberlain, 36-7
    contribution to post-war policy work, 34
    fails to address dangers of inflation, 74
    opposes incomes policies, 63-4, 73
    reform of the Party, 28
    role in post-war CRD, 33-4

Macmillan, Harold
    benefits from CRD work on housing, 109
    praises Butler's policy work, 31

Major, John
    faces unreconstructed Labour Party, 98

Maude, Angus
    CRD Chairman, 83
    manifesto writing in 1978/9, 89

Maudling, Reggie
    Chairman of Advisory Committee on Policy, 60
    character of, 59
    Churchill and, 35
    fails to address dangers of inflation, 73-4
    policy exercise of the late 1960s, 58-9
    work in post-war CRD, 33-4, 34-5

Monetarism, 72

Mortgage cap proposal, 91

Mount, Ferdinand
    on Powell romance, 32

N
Neave, Airey, 87

Newton, Tony
    'cost of living proposals', 72
    denationalisation group, 61

O
Osborne, George
    2007 Party Conference, 103

O'Shaughnessy, James
    CRD under Cameron, 101-6

Ottawa Conference, 18

P
Pakenham, Frank (*see* Longford, Earl of)

Patten, Chris
    advertising campaigns, 89
    arrives in CRD, 66-7
    CRD / CPS relations, 85
    CRD policy work after 1974, 86-90
    early recollections of Thatcher, 79-80
    preparing 1979 manifesto, 89-90
    October 1974 election, 81
    reform of local government taxation, 91-2

speech-writing, 96
Thatcher's approach to policy-making, 87

Parris, Matthew
    CRD 'louche', 93

Peel, Sir Robert
    influence on post-war policy-making, 41

Percy, Lord Eustace,
    CRD stop-gap, 9

Policy Exchange, 2

Poll tax, 91-2

Powell, Enoch
    'beyond the pale' in the late 1960s, 64
    incomes policies, 59
    most famous of CRD romances, 32, 109
    policy proposals on India, 34
        :Wales, 34
    work in post-war CRD, 33-4

Powell, Pam (née Wilson)
    CRD ' such fun', 44
    making the Brigadier smile, 32
    visit to Churchill, 44
    work on 1950 election manifesto, 44

Property-owning democracy, 49

R
Railways, 45

Reading, Brian
    'cost of living proposals', 72
    work on economic policy in the late 1960s, 65,74

Reece, Gordon, 89

Regional policy,
    pioneered by Chamberlain, 13

Ridley, Adam, 84 ,85, 93

Ridley, Nick
    denationalisation group, 61

Right Approach, 88

Right Approach to the Economy, 89

Right Road for Britain, 43-4

S

Sandys, Duncan
    Churchill's choice for CRD chairman, 29

Schreiber, Mark
    machinery of government proposals, 70

Scotland, 34, 60

Selsdon Park Conference, 68

Sewill, Brendon
    CRD in the late 1960s, 56-8
    delivers programme to Heath after 1970 election, 69
    failure of Heath's economic policies, 71-7
    1966 election manifesto, 59
    policy exercise of the late 1960s, 58-62
    relations with Heath, 56, 58-9, 66, 73-4
    Selsdon Park Conference, 68
    undergraduate CRD project, 35

Sherbourne, Stephen
    arrival in CRD, 67

Skelton, Noel
    originator of the property-owning democracy idea, 49

Spearman, Diana, 37

Social services
    post-war, 42
    CRD policy work in the late 1960s, 61-2

Special Areas Act, 13

Spicer, Michael
    recruiting for 1960s' policy work, 58

Stannard, Henry
    irreverence of, 14

Stebbings, Oliver, 57

T

Tapsell, Peter
    Butler's 'delightful chats', 37-8

Tariffs,
    reintroduction, 16-17

Tax credits, 62

Thatcher, Margaret
    avoids detailed blueprint in Opposition, 87
    continuity with Heath, 68, 72
    CRD in the 1980s, 96
    Europe, 87
    interest in ideas, 80
    'no love for the Research Department', 69
    policy work in the late 1970s, 86-90
    political skill of, 88
    reform of local government taxation, 91-2
    relations with CRD before 1974, 79-80
    Social Priorities Working Group, 61
    tax credits, 62
    trade union reform, 90

Thorneycroft, Peter, 90
    trade union reform, 86

Timothy, Nick, 104

Trade union reform, 70, 85-6

Travers, Tony
    local government expert, 92

True, Nick, 93
    CRD / CPS liaison meetings, 85

W
Wealth tax, 60-1

Wolff, Michael, 65, 80

Woolton, Lord
    house-building target, 46
    poor relations with Butler, 43
    unhappy at lack of control over CRD, 30

'Workers' Charter', 41

Worth, Sean, 106

Wyndham, John
    quoted, 95